RIVERS REMEMBER

Krupa Ge is a writer based in Madras. Her reportage and cultural writings have appeared in *The Hindu, Firstpost* and *The New Indian Express,* among other Indian and international publications over the last thirteen years. In 2017, she won a Laadli Award for a weekly column on women in cinema, 'Ms. Representation'. She was awarded the Toto-Sangam Residency Fellowship for the year 2016, and was shortlisted for a Toto Prize in Creative Writing the same year. She is also currently dabbling in screenwriting. *Rivers Remember,* her debut book, was published in 2019 by Context. *What We Know About Her* (Context, 2021), her first novel, was longlisted for the JCB Prize for Literature.

Praise for *Rivers Remember: The Shocking Truth of a Manmade Flood*

'[An] absolute must read. Well written and carefully researched, it brings home the full horror of the catastrophe. This is what the future holds for many cities around the world.'

– Amitav Ghosh, on Twitter

'Weaving together Krupa's own harrowing experience of the floods with that of others whose lives were forever changed, *Rivers Remember* also meticulously traces the why and how of what happened. Taut and incisive, this is a cautionary tale that serves to remind us we can only abuse nature so much, while telling the larger story of how urban planning works across India.'

– Anita Nair

'Chennai's history, tradition, culture and people are vital to the idea of a rich, diverse India. [...] Combining historical documents, first-person accounts, interviews and government reports, this painstakingly researched book makes an important contribution to keeping such memories alive.'

– Arvind Subramanian (Former Chief Economic Advisor)

'A powerful book that speaks truth to power, and such important reading in a city where life is wedded to its water history.'

– Meena Kandasamy, on Twitter

'The Cooum, Adayar and Kosasthalayar rivers carry within their dark waters the future, present and the past of their city—Chennai. In December 2015, that city drowned. From deep within those unforgiving waters, Krupa Ge recovers stories, memories and truths [...] Through this telling, she warns us of a dystopian future where 2015 comes to stay, even as the death knell gets louder.'

– T.M. Krishna

Reviews

'In a powerful, poetic narrative that moves between individual stories and the story of a city's drowning, Ge describes the unspeakable hollowing out of lives.'

– Uma Mahadevan Dasgupta, *The Indian Express*

'It is this job of contributing to the cultural memory of the disastrous Chennai floods of December 2015 that Krupa Ge's book does with deceptive simplicity and barely suppressed rage.'

– Nisha Susan, *Firstpost*

'I was more struck yet by how simply and movingly it documents something that's very little written about—our own ordinary, shifting, inadequate but real emotional battle to come to terms with what is happening to us.'

– Supriya Nair, *Mumbai Mirror*

'Ge's work is that rare slow reportage that could be instructive to multiple stakeholders in present-day India if they allowed it to be. It's one of the strongest works of narrative non-fiction to come out of India recently—elevating reportage with nuanced, evenkeeled writing that tells the story of a place as much as of an event.'

– Urvashi Bahuguna, *Open*

'A touching story about the people who suffered, rendered, at times lyrically, poetic as a gently flowing river, and then, with cold facts, cold as the waters that swirled the muck into homes.'

– Ramya Kannan, *The Hindu*

'Piecing together the collective failure of the authorities to protect its inhabitants from an avoidable tragedy in Chennai, Krupa Ge brings to life the agony of the trapped in a touching account of those unforgiving waters of the city rivers, relentless in reclaiming their rights over their course in *Rivers Remember*.'

– Sudhirender Sharma, *Hindustan Times*

'Elegantly blends reflections, reportage, slices from history and moving personal accounts of several of those who suffered the tragedy.'

– M.R. Venkatesh, *The Asian Age*

'For the sake of creating awareness of ground realities among the people, may the tribe of those nameless auditors who studied the Chennai Floods 2015 under the CAG of India and wrote an eminently valuable stand-alone report, as well as of authors like Krupa Ge, grow.'

– Himanshu Upadhyaya, *Citizen Matters*

'This book holds valuable lessons for people everywhere.'

– B.R.P. Bhaskar, *The Tribune*

'Amartya Sen has asserted in his writings that famines cannot occur in countries with a free press. After reading Ms Ge's book, we can also assert that floods cannot occur in a country with a free press—and the absence of one makes us vulnerable.'

– Uttaran Das Gupta, *Business Standard*

'*Rivers Remember* is a book that every Chennai vaasi must read—Krupa's fierce love for the city shines through its pages. It leaves one feeling uneasy, with the author's meticulous, data-backed research warning us that the root causes of the flood still hang over our heads like the Sword of Damocles.'

– Varsha Venugopal, *Madras Musings*

Praise for Krupa Ge's debut novel, *What We Know About Her*
Longlisted for the JCB Prize for Literature 2021
Shortlisted for the inaugural Women Writer's Prize

'With an assured yet quiet voice Krupa Ge brings forth a novel that is rich and layered in domestic history. The book is also a mirror of how memory is constructed, that it is not just the milestones but the smaller nuances that make it memorable. With a voice that is whip smart, this book achieves a lot without being noisy.'

– The JCB Prize for Literature 2021 Jury

'Like the sea that borders its beloved city of Chennai, Krupa Ge's *What We Know About Her* is a work of tides. It's about the push and pull between love and freedom, friendship and aloneness, parents and children, music and noise. It vividly recreates the vast landscapes and small worlds of Chennai and Benares, worlds apart from each other but bound by a beautiful and particular modern Indian cosmopolitanism. Above all, it gives us a cast of characters so loveable and skilfully created that it hardly seems possible they don't exist. Here is a beautiful, ambitious debut, a book for everyone who understands that the past lives on in us, as a story and sometimes as a song.'

– Supriya Nair, Writer and Editor

'Krupa Ge was born to write and pin readers to the page. Her writing has spirit, presence, kickassery you want to bottle and snort. Few write about cities, people, and fallibilities, as well as she does'

– Deepak Unnikrishnan, Author of *Temporary People*

'Really enjoyed reading this novel, which was reminiscent, in part, of Jennifer Makumbi's *The First Woman*, and also does one of my favourite things: telling a story through letters.'

– Gautam Bhatia, Author of *The Wall*

Reviews

'Steeped in memory, social commentary, curiosity, and Carnatic music Krupa Ge's *What We Know About Her* is a fiction debut to be cherished.'

– Hansda Sowvendra Shekhar, *National Herald*

'Her debut novel is also charged by her confident storytelling, along with her ability to illuminate the intersections of caste, class and gender, especially in the lives of people who are loathe to reckon with these uncomfortable truths.'

– Somak Ghoshal, *Mint Lounge*

'When I think of how my life will be chronicled by future generations, I suspect (and hope) that some aspects of our lives will be deemed regressive in the same manner we regard those before us. Yet I also hope that the women in my life are not painted as victims, but in the rich shades Krupa Ge affords to her characters.'

– Gayathri Sankar, Scroll.in

'What Krupa Ge has achieved in her debut novel *What We Know About Her* is a depiction of reality without boundaries. There are only transitions in the form of prose. The novel defies classification; it has no lines. Yet, if you were to ask what the book is about the unequivocal answer would be, "women". The novel is a tender depiction of Indian women and their agency.'

– Percy Bharucha, *Hindustan Times*

'... unputdownable. I finished the book so fast, like I was devouring a tasty burger, one big bite after another ... Kudos to Ge for creating a bunch of likeable characters. The story moves like a gently flowing river, aided by the cool breeze of Ge's writing.'

– Rachna Chhabria, *Asian Age*

'Krupa Ge's debut novel is about making journeys. The journey of unravelling the truth, the journey is in time too, from the past to the present and back, especially through the letters written by the protagonist—Yamuna's grandmother to her grandfather. It is a journey even in terms of geography, particularly between the two cities which have their own character in the novel—Chennai and Banaras. She depicts the journey of the struggles of the women... belonging to three generations... Consequently, it also becomes a journey of the self.'

– Jennifer Monteiro, *The Book Review*

MAP OF CHENNAI, 1914

KRUPA GE

RIVERS REMEMBER

#CHENNAIRAINS

and the Shocking Truth of a Manmade Flood

entxt

cntxt

First published in hardback by Context, an imprint of Westland Publications Private Limited, in 2019

First published in paperback by Context, an imprint of Westland Books, a division of Nasadiya Technologies Private Limited, in 2023

No. 269/2B, First Floor, 'Irai Arul', Vimalraj Street, Nethaji Nagar, Allappakkam Main Road, Maduravoyal, Chennai 600095

ISBN: 9789395073608

10 9 8 7 6 5 4 3 2 1

The views and opinions expressed in this work are the author's own and the facts are as reported by her, and the publisher is in no way liable for the same.

Typeset by Jojy Philip in Adobe Jenson Pro, New Delhi 110 015
Printed at Gopsons Papers Pvt. Ltd, Noida

To the people who died in the floods of 2015 in my homeland Tamil Nadu.

To my parents, Revathi and Ekambaram, who lost invaluable things and a home that December to the floods.

These people of Madras appeared really to enjoy their simple existence in town and country alike. In no part of India was a population encountered which, as far as passing observation goes, seemed to be so quietly glad to exist under the common conditions of human life.

—Edwin Arnold, *India Revisited*, 1886

Contents

Prologue

'How On Earth Did This Happen to Us?'[i]

My parents were asleep when it started. In a matter of minutes, nearly six feet of water filled up their home. If a neighbour hadn't alerted them, they would have gone under, along with their house. They lost everything that night to the city's rivers.

In December 2015, floods ravaged the coastal southern Indian town I call home—Chennai. There was chaos, death and heartbreak. Most importantly, floods were no longer something that happened to someone else in the news.

Questions gnawed away at me in the aftermath of that disastrous night, even as I felt helpless and sorry for myself. Why hadn't the government warned my parents? Were there others like them? Why was nobody held responsible for this obvious failure?

Around the time of the floods, I read Haruki Murakami's *Underground*. It is a complex and compelling non-fictional account of the sarin gas attack in the Tokyo subway. Murakami was inspired to write this book after reading a letter in a magazine, in which the wife of a victim asks: 'How on earth did this happen to us?' I could relate to this question, a lot. By August 2016, I had a clear vision for this book. I wanted to capture the events that unfolded that night by interviewing victims from across the city, cutting across social barriers. There were also other questions that needed answers. Why did Chennai flood? Was it really because of a 'once-in-a-hundred-year rain' as the authorities claimed? Why didn't they prepare for this eventuality despite warnings of heavy rains? Why weren't people evacuated? Why was there no warning? Why wasn't the state government forthcoming about how many people had died? Why did the national media in India ignore this news until it was too late?

These questions were important to me at a personal level too because of what had happened to my parents. But floods aren't just personal. They don't happen to one family.

I spent over three years, between December 2015 and May 2019, interviewing victims and volunteers of the Chennai floods, looking through historical archives of our rivers and their fates, filing RTI queries and appeals, reading through government proposals and state disaster management plans, following court proceedings on various Public Interest Litigations—on the floods, encroachments on water bodies and eviction of the poor from their homes on river banks—and speaking to journalists who covered the floods for news organisations.

My conversations and investigations uncovered that the floods of 2015 in Chennai were a manmade disaster; that the Tamil Nadu (TN) government had played an undeniable role in drowning clueless citizens without any warning; that it had also played an active role in sabotaging the city's water bodies over the years; that our government agencies are just not equipped to deal with the kind of calamities we are struck by, from the tsunami to heavy rainfall like that of 2015 and powerful cyclones; that we are a vulnerable people and our disaster management skills are unsophisticated and poor; that the 'tyranny of distance'[ii] is real and it affects how seriously the nation takes our catastrophes.

A bigger picture too began to emerge as I dug deeper into this crisis. In the time that it took to write this book, there have been heavy floods in the USA, in the UK and Ireland (all in December 2015), Peru (2016–2017), across Europe (2018), East Africa (2018), south-western Japan (2018) and in the southern Indian state of Kerala (2018) closer to home. Floods are commonplace now, and frequent too. This cocktail of coasts, cyclones, floods and rains is made deadlier by the undeniable reality of climate change.

In India, dams and reservoirs pose huge problems and risks. Apart from legal tussles and bitter acrimony between states over the sharing of river water, and the invariable displacement of the poor, these structures also cause flooding. Floods and droughts—two sides of the same coin—come in succession to haunt our poor who depend largely on water for agriculture. The year 2016–17, for instance, saw severe droughts across TN.

After suffering tremendous personal loss, I needed to know if my trauma could have been averted. If the loss of lives, livelihoods and resources across the state could have been avoided. I found out, to my utter disbelief, that it indeed could have been if the authorities had acted. I was appalled to find out that Chennai city's largest source of water, the Chembarambakkam Reservoir, which also drowned us that December, follows a three-decade-old rule book for flood management. And that even after the floods, TN state officials showed no interest in updating the flood guidelines for the reservoirs. There isn't even a mention of it in the latest disaster management plan for TN (2018–2030). The state, which has seen some of the worst natural disasters from tsunami (2005) to cyclones (Ockhi in 2017), is yet to demonstrate that it is ready to handle future catastrophes. The other states in the country don't seem to fare any better.

If you live in urban India and find your home and your city sinking, it's possibly because of the mismanagement of water bodies; because rivers remember. My parents' home sank without any warning. No one else's should.

Notes

i. Haruki Murakami, *Underground: The Tokyo Gas Attack and the Japanese Psyche*, Vintage, 2003.

ii. Rajdeep Sardesai, 'TN Floods and the Tyranny of Distance', Breaking View, 10 December 2015, rajdeepsardesai.net.

A Part of Our Home Dies

1 December 2015, Chennai

Social media is rife with rumours about a flood. Stories of crocodiles escaping from the Madras Crocodile Bank, a rumour that also did the rounds during the tsunami, are back on WhatsApp. This time, it is accompanied by grainy photographs and news clippings that look at least a decade old. I know these are not true, but something else creeps up on me: a palpable fear of flooding, especially the neighbourhood my parents live in.

I call my father, and he assures me there's nothing to worry about, because their home—even though only a few hundred metres away from Satya Nagar, which is on the banks of the Adyar River and often goes under water during heavy rains—has never flooded. In any case, cement bags filled with sand have been readied, my father says, so that bunds may be raised to prevent any water from coming in. I am not entirely convinced, but I have no reason to believe that my childhood home will flood. We agree to stay in touch and to keep our phones fully charged while the power lasts.

Soon enough, there's a blackout across most parts of the city, including the T Nagar area, where my spouse Swaroop and I live. We have been so worried about waters entering my parents' home that we have forgotten to store water in ours. As the power goes off and the water pump stops working, we realise we have run out of water. Not a drop around, either in a bottle or a bucket.

We tie ropes to buckets and draw water from the underground tank outside our apartment and carry them over to our house. We spend as little of it as we can. Every resource is maximised. A frugality that harks back to a different era. We try to stay off the internet to save power on our cell phones and ration our social media usage, even as information deficit envelopes us in an eerie silence. I post, on Instagram, what I think is a stupid, yet bizarrely accurate photograph of my feelings. A miniature human toy hanging on to dear life from the inside edge of a filled wine glass. I caption it: 'Things are looking a bit grim here.' We try to read to get over our fears. Swaroop is reading R. Nath's *Private Life of Mughals in India* and I am reading Haruki Murakami's *Underground*.

My brother and sister-in-law, Balajee and Subadra, who live a little away from our home, are on battle mode too. They switch their phones on by turns, and that too only to check on all of us and to look for signs of emergency. They seem ready for whatever might be thrown their way.

They live in a first-floor apartment, and their car is parked on the ground floor. Their home too, like ours, is tucked away on a quiet street, removed from too much noise and traffic but still right in the middle of the city. It is colourful and filled with artefacts and artwork that Subadra, a self-taught artist, is working on just then. They too are trying to make the most of what is available, rationing backup lights and fans.

Back in my parents' home, my mother too, like all of us, has an odd sort of feeling in her stomach. Unlike any of us, however, she isn't really waiting for anything to happen to her. While my father tries to reconnect with the world outside, looking for scraps and bits of information on the internet, she is busy packing. But how does one pack twenty years of one's life and into what? Where does one go for boxes large enough and how does one know how much time one has?

My parents' house is compact. At approximately 650 square feet, it is a typical Chennai flat on the ground floor of a three-storeyed building. It is home to Hindus, Muslims, Tamils, Telugus, Punjabis, Sourashtrians, Kannadigas and, until some time ago, to the last of the area's Anglo Indians. The building had always been robust and mixed, even before my parents moved in twenty-five years ago. And this diversity has only got better with time. The south-facing living room wears a dark, cool and sometimes gloomy look, even in the afternoons when the rest of the city is parched, dry and hot. From the street, when the apartment's door is open, you can see right through the living room, to the kitchen, and then through the kitchen windows into the building behind, and further down, to my mother's older sister's house.

The kitchen doubles up as the prayer room and is lined with idols, photos and holy collectables from all over—Varanasi, Vatican and Mecca. My mother is a believer and a Madras-bred secular gal. The food in that kitchen is magical: thick, tangy kozhambu, melt-in-your-mouth potato curry, and the best rasam in town. It heals when you are sick, invigorates when you are down and it lulls you to sleep on Sunday afternoons. No matter what she makes, it tastes like comfort food. My father too is a wonderful cook; his dal is unparalleled.

My parents' home has two bedrooms, two bathrooms—one Indian and one western—and mosaic tile flooring that is cool all through the year. The open lofts are filled with my grandmother's utensils, and diaries and notes left behind by my communist grandfather, who founded the Cine Musicians Union of Madras. In there, also live dolls wrapped in bits of old torn dhotis and sarees, which come down only once a year to be displayed during the nine-day Navratri festival, Golu.

There isn't space for too much furniture, but every nook has been optimised to its fullest. There are shelves nailed to wall corners, a showcase on the wall that can be reached only if one stands on the long, brown stool that's been around for as long as my parents have been married. There's a hexagonal dining table in the living room. There's a three-seater sofa in wood, with red- and gold-coloured cushions and a diwan made in Andhra, where my father used to work. There are a few plastic chairs, a bed made in Tirupati from back when my parents were a young couple, and a computer table on which sits a good old-fashioned personal computer. There's an LED TV lent by a friend. And memories, oh, so many of them, in the form of knick-knacks strewn all around the house.

There are cooking utensils in the open shelves of the kitchen that have stayed in the family for over thirty years and heirloom pots passed on from my grandmother—most of them stainless steel, some of them bronze. There are two steel bureaus, one of them as old as my parents' marriage and the other bought to accommodate my brother Balajee's and my clothes. The older bureau is filled with sarees, some silk and over fifty years old, and many chiffons. Its locker is home to all of my parents' secrets, ones my brother and I are only quasi-privy too, ones that my mother guards. It's not filled with money or gold, really. They are just papers—receipts, correspondences and the like. Lots and lots of it, collected over the years.

So how does one begin to wrap all of this, one's labour of love, one's home, bundle them up and carry them over to safety, when one has no warning or no knowledge of what is to come?

While my father keeps a vigil to check if water levels are rising and by how much, my mother rounds up anything that can become a container—a large blue barrel with a black lid that they keep around to store water during the horrid water shortage that hits Chennai every year between March and June; buckets, so many of them; and dhotis and sarees.

She throws papers, whatever she can lay her hands on or thinks is important, into the barrel, and with the help of two young boys, her neighbours, carries them up to the first floor of the building into someone else's home. She gathers all the silk sarees in a dhoti and sends them up. She grabs everything small, valuable and easily packable, and begins to put them away, when my father finally chips in to help my mother, half-convinced, while Swaroop and I wait in our house and Balajee and Subadra wait in theirs for news.

My mother now takes a torch and walks around the apartment building, wading through the darkness that has engulfed the entire street. It is pitch dark and she's alone. She shines the torch along the drains. She sees dark, large insects crawling up and down the pipes and stays far away, but would wonder later if she had imagined them in the darkness and if the shadows had played a trick on her. She is auditing the water level in the drain sumps of the building. She goes home and removes the covers from the drains and checks on the water levels there. She's convinced that the waters are going to come in, and that they are going to come in through the drains. She's convinced when no one else is even anticipating it. She walks around restless. She chats with neighbours. Everyone's worried, their furrowed faces lit by candles, by now the only source of light. There's no backup power anywhere.

There's darkness. There's silence. There's fear. There's a creeping sense of discomfort in the air, which is new to those of us cushioned till now by the privileges of the salaried class. For others like my mother, forgetfulness comes in handy, for Chennai has witnessed floods every few decades (1903, 1943, 1978, 1985 and 2002). But there's also a renewed sense of camaraderie among the people of the building. A quiet understanding that makes it alright. Offers have come from those who live in the upper floors: 'If you need anything, don't hesitate to ask.' 'Come sleep in our home if something happens.' 'Would you like a cup of tea or something?'

After a lot of thinking, worrying, wondering, chatting with people in the apartment, accompanied by nervous laughter, my parents go to sleep. They try to sleep. A very light slumber that dances around wakefulness descends, as if it knows something is coming.

~

2 December 2015

At 4 a.m., there's an urgent knock on the door.

'Aunty! Aunty!' Manoj, our young neighbour calls.

Amma opens the door.

'Water's entered our house. It's rising steadily,' he says.

'It hasn't come here, pa,' Amma says. Before she can get her bearings and look for her glasses, it begins.

Water gushes in from the kitchen's and bathroom's drains as well as from the road. A quick human chain is formed in that darkness, as black, sludge-filled water that has mingled with waste from the sewers by this point, starts to fill up my parents' home. More things Amma spent the night packing are quickly transported up the stairs.

Just as they prepare to leave the house, my mother says to my father, 'Go get the rice. We can't let so many kilos of it rot.'

My father tries to go back in, but the water is unexpectedly slippery and he almost falls. He tries to go in again, and then gives up. My parents and the young boys of the building are now debating if they must lock the house or not.

How do you decide what's best for your house when it's filling up with 'water' that has come up almost to your neck? Do you just close the door? Do you lock it? Do you leave it open? Will the water go away if you leave it open? Or will it still stay inside?

A million questions zip through his mind but there are only a few seconds left. Appa shuts the door and as the greasy water threatens to drown him, he fumbles but eventually manages to lock it.

He wades through the water and joins Amma on the first floor.

~

I get a call from an unknown landline number.

Groggy and still in bed, I pick up the phone.

'Hello.'

'It's me,' my father says. I spring up from the mattress.

'Are you okay? Where are you?'

'Water entered the house last night. Around 4 a.m. We are safe, don't worry. We are upstairs on the third floor.'

My heart breaks a little as his words slowly register. 'We are coming there to get you, okay?'

'The water's come up to the first floor, almost. Impossible for us to go down or for anyone to come in. Anyway, we are on the third floor now. Don't worry. Water can't possibly come all the way up here,' he says reassuringly.

'Is the house okay?'

'Hmm. I don't know.'

'Are you okay?'

'We are actually having a decent time. So many of us together in the building, right? So it's all good.'

'I asked you to come, right? Why didn't you just leave then?'

'If we hadn't stayed, we would have never been able to save as much as we did.'

'What?'

'Yeah. Your mother saved all that's important. The furniture and stuff, I don't know what's going to happen with that. But everything else is fine.'

'Oh.'

'Look, this is the only phone working and we are able to make calls but not receive. You can try reaching me on this but I am not sure if it will work. Don't worry about us. We are fine.' And then, he's gone.

I open Facebook and write, 'Marooned in T Nagar while my parents' home flooded at 4 a.m. Beyond frustrating. Endless suckfest.'

~

After waiting around all morning, looking out the window, watching the water levels go up and down and then almost reach our ground-floor apartment—which, thankfully, is a few feet higher than the road—Swaroop and I have had enough. We charge our phones in his car parked just outside the apartment, and are thinking of taking it out and going ... somewhere. Anywhere.

His red A-Star car, which Swaroop has nicknamed Saroja (because roja, or rose, is red), had been our companion through the first half of that November. We were on a road trip, from Chennai to Kanyakumari. We passed through Pondicherry, Tranquebar, Nagore, Vailankanni, Sikkal, Tanjore, Tuticorn, Manapad, Kanyakumari and Madurai. We missed the rains by a whisker in many of these places; just as we left a town, we would receive a call from my father about flash flood warnings. The rains finally caught up with us as we drove back home from Madurai to Chennai. It poured so heavily that we could see nothing on the highway, and it was sheer luck that kept us going. The car's wipers fought hard, but all we could see that night was sheets of water as if we were standing behind a waterfall. When we hit the outskirts of Chennai, we were sure the car would stop moving. The roads were inundated heavily around Tambaram, through which we had to enter the central part of the city, where we live. Saroja held on admirably, and we reached home safe on 15 November, two days before the first round of widespread flooding in the city. My own car, a gold-coloured Alto that I bought with my journalist's salary on EMI—I had vowed to buy myself a car after having swallowed abuse at the hands of men on public transport all through my childhood, shrinking with rage and shame—is back in my parents' house, *safe*, far away from the basement car park of my building.

We get a call at around two in the afternoon from Hredai, Swaroop's cousin, who lives not far away. He says there's no flooding anywhere near his home and that he has power, and there's no sign of distress at all. He threatens to wade in to give us supplies. So we decide to go to him instead.

We shake it off, whatever it was that was holding us back and get into Swaroop's car. We reach the main road, under the GN Chetty Road flyover in the heart of Chennai and I am almost certain the car is going to stop, because there's just water everywhere. It enters the car and reaches our ankles. We drive through the water and try to comfort each other. People are rushing to places. Cars have stopped in the middle of the road and are beginning to float a bit; that's how much water there is. The water inside our car is steadily rising and almost hits our knees.

We reach Cathedral Road, barely a kilometre away from our home, and are stung by the realisation that not everything in the city is drowning. We feel betrayed. Some roads seem to be holding up. And we are shocked by just how normal things are by the time we reach TTK Road in Alwarpet, barely three and a half kilometres from home.

'For a while, we felt guilty that we had power and there was no flooding here. We switched everything off. Because how do you react to something like this?' Hredai asks us when we reach his place in the evening.

I charge my phone and try to reach my parents.

Nothing.

I then make some plain instant noodles and eat. Dinner for desperate times.

'People are stocking up on war footing. Milk, eggs, bread, what have you. Instant noodles seemed like the best option to us for times like this,' our host says.

I try calling Balajee and can't reach him either. I tweet asking for information on Srinagar Colony, where my parents live and is about six kilometres away from Hredai's house. I run a search for it on Twitter—hundreds of 'unable to reach my parents' posts from anxious children, just like me, show up. I put my phone on charge and go to sleep on comfortable mattresses spread out for us on the floor, and wait.

We would learn later that the previous night, Balajee and Subadra had watched a nightmare unfold in their first-floor flat.

~

My brother and sister-in-law watch from their balcony as water rises steadily, because of the Mambalam Canal, which has till then, for all practical purposes, only been known as some sort of a sewer to most of us in the city. (It is only after the flood I would learn that the Mambalam Canal runs right through GN Chetty Road, few metres from my home as well.)

The two of them watch the water rise every few minutes. It goes from ankle deep, to knee deep and then, the cars in the building begin to float. Later, the cars are submerged completely. They are bewildered because it's so gradual. Of all of us, they have the worst night in some ways because they keep thinking the water will recede any minute now. It is dark, so they can see only what the narrow beam of the torch illuminates. Their own car begins to float. And then my brother's old bike, which has been with him for over a decade, disappears under the water.

All through the night, car alarms keep going on and off. They sound like trapped animals crying for help. Their neighbours on the ground floor, just like my parents, caught unaware, drop everything and run to the first floor. Everything valuable, everything dear, just left as is inside their home. They too eat instant noodles and try to rest but sleep eludes them.

~

Swaroop and I spend the day hanging by the phone, trying to think up ways to combat this sense of gloom.

Nothing.

It has been a ridiculously dull day and we try our best to stay away from social media. It's addictive. We post about my parents and ask if someone has gone to the area on a rescue boat to check in on the elderly, who live by the hordes there. It's funny how overnight we are just as helpless as the hundreds of NRI kids trying desperately to reach their parents or find out about them. It's funny how the floods can shrink the distance between the USA, UK, UAE and TTK Road and can place a distance the size of a continent between TTK Road and Srinagar Colony. It's funny how in this age of information—when all we have to do is scroll down Facebook timelines and WhatsApp chat windows for updates from the people we love, cherish, loathe and stalk—a blackout of this nature can drive us to the brink of insanity. We refresh our feeds on Facebook, hit search on Google, search for hashtags on Twitter and look just about everywhere for news of our loved ones, for any news at all. It's as if an addict has been asked to go cold turkey. Add to this the fact that most of the people that are trapped are unable to come online and post updates, while their families, we, are online, creating a network of hysteria. As if the only way to show we care is by being hysterical. Sometimes, maybe it is.

In the evening at around 4, I receive a call from Balajee. I am jumpy again. We are unable to connect to the network well. The call keeps dropping and frustration threatens to break me.

Finally, the call connects. Balajee and Subadra are safe. They have waded through neck-deep water (and by water I mean the same sewer water that besieged my parents' home). Like us, they too didn't want to wait alone in their apartment any longer, and want to meet us. They have run out of water and food. They are on Venkatanarayana Road, which is on one side of Chennai's lifeline, Anna Salai. This main road runs from the northern end of the city near the Cooum River, all the way to the south-western part, Guindy, across the Adyar.

Swaroop and I make it to Chamiers Road, which is on the other side of the historic Anna Salai. We are separated by a few metres, yet unable to cross the road. There, on Anna Salai, at that spot called Nandanam Signal, which at that time of the day would usually be teeming with vehicles and hundreds of humans, now has floodwaters gushing through it. Ferociously. So bad is the situation that we see army personnel, with ropes tied across the road, trying to transport people. Even they aren't sure what to do. Our hearts sink. Our calls stop connecting. We stare at the waters before retreating in defeat.

Later in the day, the two wade through more water and make it to Subadra's maternal home, two kilometres away from us in Gopalapuram, another area untouched by the floods, and we meet them there.

~

3 December 2015

I receive a call from my father saying their building is no longer flooded. Water has receded and everyone is safe. We want to go across, but there's no way for us to reach them because the main roads are still marooned and all access into the colony is cut off. Once we know they are out of the woods, we are a wee bit relieved. We go to a small shop in Gopalapuram, Pickwick Silkhouse, and buy new clothes. It hadn't even occurred to us to pack.

~

5 December 2015

Two excruciatingly slow, painful days have passed. As waters recede, we go to my parents' home. The city wears a look of despair and absolute disarray. Eerie, murky and nothing like the Chennai we have grown up in for three decades now. The poor stand in queues on roads, as buses filled with volunteers distribute aid. Those rendered homeless, as their homes have been washed away, take whatever comes their way—sarees, nighties, hot homemade food, buckets, dhotis, lungis, mineral water bottles, sanitary napkins, mosquito repellents—sometimes running behind vans and cars that have run out of supplies. These are some of the most hardworking people, the working class of the city. Memories of their arms extended for food, clothes and water bottles would remain etched in our minds, for a long time after the flood. This is especially painful to watch as food security has been among the biggest success stories of Tamil Nadu (TN).

The tree-lined streets around my parents' home, where I learned to cycle and where carpets of flowers from kondrai trees that find mention in the Tamil poems of the glorious Sangam era welcome me usually, looks like a giant garbage dump. Despair grips me as I wonder how this city is ever going to recover from this.

Then we open my childhood home. And it looks like a war was fought in there. A battle with the Adyar River.

What no one tells you about floods like this is that it is not water that comes into your home. Let me tell you now once and for all so when it happens to you—and happen it will, for our cities are not flood resilient—you can be prepared. Floods are the new norm, everywhere in the world. And what flows into your home when it floods, is sewage. Almost always. Mostly human waste, but also other waste.

The floor of our home has a thick layer of sludge, and upon it, my mother who's eager to walk in and see her home, however bad its shape might be, falls. Our hearts stop for a few seconds, before she gets up and marches on.

Everything looks black, as if someone brought a lorry full of sludge from a gutter and meticulously smeared every single item in the house with it—stainless steel utensils, mattresses, bedsheets, pillows, nooks and crannies filled with trinkets that have built up over twenty years, photographs of gods, grandparents, idols, buckets, mugs, papers, oh, so many. No piece of furniture is in its place. The gas cylinder has moved out of the kitchen and is next to the entrance. The fridge is on its side. The washing machine upside down. And the house stinks. A stench that is unbearable and unlike anything we have ever experienced. Our beautiful home is destroyed. Everything is gone. The home we grew up in, that sheltered us from rains and the hot Chennai sun, where countless life events happened, things built and bought over years, life savings, a lifetime of everything, an entire way of life, is gone. Unable to bring ourselves to do anything, or say anything to anyone, we leave. In silence. To come back another day. On the way out I see my car. My father's left its doors open to dry it out. Fungus has taken over the interiors. It smells rotten. It is no longer the golden chariot I knew. It is all but metal scrap now and will never run again. I will never hold that steering wheel in my hands and feel grateful for the chances that came my way.

We will rebuild our parents' home, no doubt. We will buy a different car, in time. Money isn't as hard to come by now as it was when we were younger. Things have changed for me. For us. But I think of the younger me and the people who are as vulnerable now as we were then. The enormity of it all. Of the images we usually see with utter indifference on television, of people running towards helicopters that drop ration on to rooftops, somewhere else, in Orissa maybe, or Andhra, during a flood, or just beyond our parents' home in Satya Nagar. Of rains lashing and water, water everywhere you turn, of words we throw around flippantly, as if it has nothing to do with us, words like flood, relief, aid, helicopters, ration, boats and rescue missions ... All this takes over our mind. Our life. Our sleep.

What I did not know then was that my parents had moved almost immediately into a neighbour's apartment on the third floor when the water had come in. Mr Chandrashekar had opened up his home to them with great generosity. They were all worried, sure, but it was with some amount of incredulousness that I heard stories of my parents having dinner by candle lights, of using rainwater for cooking or drinking, and a production line of idlis in one neighbour's kitchen for over a dozen people marooned in nearly six feet of water and with nowhere to go.

A Part of Their Home Survives

We didn't think they'd remember. But they did. They remembered their many homes, every single one they had breathed in before, thrived in. It was as if nothing had changed. As if someone had turned the clock back. Their ancient homes looked different now, but once they started to make their way in, they claimed it as their own, again.

You see, we had thought of them as but minor obstacles to building a bustling metropolis. We displaced them, disallowed them from entering their own turf. And then we built on top of their homes. They had been around for long, for as long as time can be. And yet we said there was no place for them in the city.

All we saw of them was their struggle for survival, the remnants of their decrepit homes, their unkempt facades and the endless barrage of mosquitoes they bred, as if to strike vengeance. When we passed by them, we covered our noses and looked away.

Then, when the skies made love to the ocean and pregnant clouds burst forth with droplets that grew slowly into raging thunderstorms, puddles turned into ponds, and then lakes. The floodgates of their memories were thrown wide open. It was time for them to come back to claim our uneven tar roads, with their bodies covered in grime, dark and brown, like syrupy jaggery and molasses.

There are three of them that call Chennai their home: the Kosasthalaiyar, the Cooum and the Adyar. Rivers. Their home survives in their memories, and they showed us its power in December 2015.

~

The ancient practice of kudimaramathu—kudi meaning people and maramathu meaning repair, wherein a village was responsible for maintaining, repairing and taking care of water bodies—died out over time. Though the TN government announced an eponymous scheme that harks back to this practice, first in 1975 and later in 2017, it has repeatedly faced hiccups,[1] with farmers complaining of monetary loss and corruption.

The waterways of yore, managed by the Tamils and the Telugus, who inhabited this city in large swathes, consisted of aaru, or river—the name Adyar actually comes from Adai-aru—and eri, or lake—like the Retteri, meaning two lakes, which receives water from the Red Hills Reservoir and the Korattur Lake. The names of many neighbourhoods in Chennai are derived from Tamil words for water bodies. The word karanai in Pallikaranai, for instance, refers to a water body, and thaangal, as in Pazhavanthaangal and Vedanthaangal, refers to irrigation tanks. There were also kulams, or ponds, in the nomenclature, like in Kolathur.

Though Chennai has retained names of ancient waterways and areas that derive their names from water, there's little glory left for these water bodies. Think of all the 'lake view apartments' that no longer enjoy views of lakes, like in the Nungambakkam area built on a lake to reclaim land for development, or the Lake View Road in Mambalam built by filling up what was once called Long Tank, which no longer exists except in historical maps and the musings of the city's historians. Long Tank used to be between the Adyar and Cooum Rivers. Powers that be, a potent mix of real estaters, politicians and policymakers, have sold us dreams of owning a piece of this big Pattanam—maritime town—by telling us that it's okay to build on marshes, lakes and poromboke lands that were reserved for shared communal uses.

They failed us. And in turn, we failed our rivers.

Where Does Our Water Come From?

Water, rather the lack of it, has always been a concern for those of us living in Chennai. Loud calls of 'thanni vandaachu' to announce the arrival of the Metro Water lorries, resound across rich and poor neighbourhoods, especially in summer.

Until the floods in 2015, I hadn't paid much attention to where our water comes from. It was only when the water had finally reached my own home, without the help of lorries, that I found out about the four large reservoirs—Puzhal (1876), Poondi (1944), Sholavaram (1876–77) and Chembarambakkam (from the Pallava era)—in suburban Chennai, which take care of the city's water needs. This is also supplemented by groundwater, desalination plants in Nemelli and Minjur in neighbouring districts, the Veeranam Tank that brings the Cauvery River's water and the Telugu Ganga Project that brings water from the Krishna River in the neighbouring Andhra Pradesh.

But one river, over all the others, even though it does not flow through the city, has captured the heads, hearts and politics of Chennai. From festivals along her banks to paeans sung in her praise, it is the Cauvery, unlike any of the city's rivers, that is on the lips of every farmer, citizen and neighbour of Tamil Nadu.

Even as Chennai battles for the Cauvery, boycotts IPL matches and engages in bitter banter over sharing water, it has ignored her sisters who call this very city home—the Adyar, Cooum and Kosasthalaiyar Rivers.

The 136-kilometre-long Kosasthalaiyar splits into two branches outside Chennai at the Kesavaram Dam. The main branch, Kosasthalaiyar, feeds the Poondi Reservoir and then flows through the Thiruvallur district. From there, it reaches the Bay of Bengal in the north of the city.

Meanwhile, the other branch, Cooum, heads south from the dam into central Chennai's Kilpauk, Nungambakkam and Triplicane areas, before heading to the Bay of Bengal.

The Adyar begins at the Chembarambakkam Reservoir, from where it travels through Kanchipuram, Thiruvallur and southern Chennai, before joining the sea near the Adyar area.

Cutting through all three major rivers is the manmade freshwater navigation channel, Buckingham Canal, built in 1806.

Chennai also has an elaborate system of natural and manmade drainage. This includes many small lakes, drains, and canals. The city's rivers, however, are seasonal and remain dry for a large part of the year. They receive excess water, if any, after feeding its reservoirs. Many people do not even realise that they are crossing rivers and canals while crossing the bridges in the city, for they look less like rivers and more like parched playgrounds, ripe for leisurely games of cricket and kite-flying, or they look like sewage canals. The 150-year-old beautiful Napier Bridge built over the Cooum near the Marina Beach has fewer admirers because of its stench. The same goes for the Periyar Bridge previously called St. George's Bridge built in 1805.

It is this very complex network of interconnected water bodies and drainage system that drowned us in December 2015, when rains lashed the city.

Major Waterways of Chennai

Waterway	*Total Length (km) – Chennai city*	*Length (km) – (Chennai Metropolitan Area)*
River Cooum	18.0	40.0
River Adyar	15.0	24.0
North Buckingham Canal	7.1	17.1
Central Buckingham Canal	7.2	7.2
South Buckingham Canal	4.2	16.1
Otteri Nullah	10.2	10.2
Captain Cotton Canal	2.9	4.0
Kosasthalaiyar	-	16.0
Mambalam Drain	9.4	9.4
Kodungaiyur Drain	6.9	6.9
Virugambakkam–Arumbakkam Drain	6.9	6.9
Total Length	23.2	157.8

Source: Chennai Metropolitan Development Authority. The Chennai Metropolitan Area (CMA) refers to Chennai city and its suburbs, Kanchipuram and Thiruvallur districts. The development of all three regions is overseen by the Chennai Metropolitan Development Authority.

How a City Went Under

Between 8 November and 11 November 2015, several parts of Tamil Nadu received 125 mm to 280 mm of rainfall every day. By mid-November, a swollen Adyar greeted people, and a nervousness was apparent. Unable to sift through the rumours and news breaks, people waited in anxiety.

The Chembarambakkam Reservoir's Full Tank Level (FTL) is 85.4 feet. By 24 November, it had water up to 83.8 feet,[2] and what had occurred a week before, on 17 November, created concern among the people of South Chennai, when 18,000 cusecs of water—over five lakh litres per second—was released from the reservoir,[3] severely flooding the neighbourhoods of West Tambaram, Mudichur, and some parts of Pammal, Anakaputhur, Manapakkam, Saidapet and Kotturpuram,[4] all on the banks of the Adyar.

Through the month of November, 1,218.6 mm of rains had pounded the city.[5] That's 1218.6 litres of rain over a square metre. To put this in perspective, the usual rainfall expected at this time of the year is less than one-third of this, around 400 mm.

However, between 24 and 30 November, the city received very little rainfall and the time was ripe for the authorities to release more water from the Chembarambakkam into the Adyar. But they did not. Even though there were predictions for heavy to very heavy rainfall during this period, the reservoir was kept at 85–88 per cent full. Newspaper reports the following week said that this holding of water between 24 and 30, despite warnings, exacerbated the situation caused by the 'once-in-a hundred-year-rain.'[6]

The city was moving unusually slowly. It was, in fact, tottering back to its routine from a really wet November. People in low-lying areas were told, 'Well, that's the price you pay for building your home on a lake,' in as many different ways as possible by city planners, social media pundits, environmentalists and politicians. Why do homes get built on lakes and tanks in Chennai? And why do people, rich and not-so-rich, move in there? The poor and marginalised do not build their homes on lakes and tanks, because they cannot afford it. They settle *around* water bodies, on their banks. And yet, when it comes to the removal of 'encroachments', they are the first in the line of fire.

On 14 November, the then chief minister J. Jayalalithaa had called the initial damage due to heavy rains in various areas 'inevitable.'[7] And so people too were telling themselves there's nothing anyone could have done. A small price to pay in the large scheme of things. For calling a piece of land your home in Chennai. The big city. Pattanam. In fact, for most of the city that lived in these low areas, flooding was a matter of routine, though this year had been extraordinarily tough.

Every year, when the rains come to Chennai, erratic and sparse as they are, many homes submerge. Nobody complains loudly and there is usually no one to complain to. The city waits for the end of the wet and debilitating November and to step into December, usually the most tolerable of months, mostly weather-wise but also otherwise, as the Tamil month of Margazhi falls in December.

'Margazhi thingal madhi niraindha nannalaal'—the month of Margazhi, filled with the light of the moon—so begins *Thiruppavai*, written by the only female Vaishnavite bhakti saint-poet Andal, and heard across Vishnu temples of Tamil Nadu this time of the year. Temple visits are re-scheduled from evenings to early mornings, and '*Margazhi thingal madi naraya pongal*' is a favourite twist on the classic song in the city—'In the Margazhi month, my lap is full of pongal'—referring to the hot pongal prasadam offered to all who step into these temples. Large kolams adorn the entrances of temples and homes, and a feeling of festivity is in the air. Carols flow out of churches, as Christmas season begins. Raisins are soaked in rum and Carnatic concerts are awaited. A large number of visitors, mostly NRIs, are expected, for the music season as well as yearly family visits during the Christmas break. For many 'eligible' young men and women living abroad, the December break is the perfect time to come back home to Chennai and look for a future spouse. They see a number of 'candidates' and mull over them until the auspicious month of Thai that begins mid-January, when marriages are aplenty.

That December, as salaries, for the lucky few that drew them towards the end of the previous month, trickled in, people were thinking of replacing furniture, mattresses and cushions that had been damaged in the floods on 17 November. Chennai wanted to relax and enjoy its most favourite month, but an unrest loomed over it. The rains seemed unrelenting.

And then it happened.

After a lull in the rainfall in the last week of November, 490 mm of rain pounded parts of the city on 1 December.[8]

Officials opened the Chembarambakkam and let 29,000 cusecs of water out into the Adyar, over a period of twelve hours. This alleged 'once-in-a-hundred-year-rain', a freak incident in one of the hottest years in Chennai, plunged the city into untold misery and wiped out the lives and livelihoods of many, even as rains continued to lash the city unabated.

On that day, the Chembarambakkam saw an inflow of 31,000 cusecs, 26,000 of it before six in the evening.[9] And as this large amount of water joined the networks of rivers and drains, which were already full because of breaches and swollen lakes, there was pandemonium.

In fury and frenzy, the Adyar engulfed parts of Chennai. One by one, homes of the rich, poor and all those in between, with palm frond roofs, Mangalore tiles, asbestos and concrete ones that are sloping and straight, cycles, cycle rickshaws, homes of musicians with nadaswarams, veenas, violins, thavils, tamburas, mridangams, keyboards, drum kits, flutes, guitars and pianos, abodes of astrologers, believers, atheists and agnostics, offices of lawyers with bundles and case notes, autorickshaws, SUVs, sedans, luxury, imported, second-hand and antique cars, mansions, hotels, hostels, factories small and large, flour mills, Bharatanatyam and Kuchipudi schools, IT parks, call centres, petty shops, tea shops, supermarkets, shops for expats stocked with condiments from Korea and Japan, seaweed and udon noodles, atho shops that sell Burmese food, police stations, playgrounds, parks, stalls laden with fruits on the sides of the roads and covered in blue tarpaulin, banks, ATMs, malls, pharmacies, trade centres, clubs of the elite, libraries filled with books old and precious, petrol bunks, bridges, highways, mud, tar, concrete, arterial and remote roads, subways, railway tracks, housing colonies, villas, far-away houses built by the slum clearance board, whole slums, apartment buildings, universities, colleges, the governor's bungalow, reserved forests, insurance offices, cows, calves, goats, dogs, cats, ducks, LPG offices filled with cylinders, hospitals filled with the dying, the pregnant and people suffering from senility, wedding halls, buildings under construction, public toilets, sign boards, name boards, MTC buses, lorries filled with wares, skin clinics, burger joints, milk depots, toll booths, schools, ration shops with sacks upon sacks of rice, wheat, dal and sugar, post offices, fishing hamlets, meen body vehicles, beef stalls, aircrafts, terrified puppies, temples ancient and new, those under trees, in T-junctions and sacred termite hills, mosques that host the wealthy and humble, churches that have been around from when Christianity first arrived in Madras and where apostles lived and breathed, mutts where seers sit, durgahs with the remains of saints, homes of priests and ministers, iron boxes and coal blocks of men and women who run ironing stalls on street footpaths, money plants, curry leaf plants and terrace gardens of retired men and women, lamp posts, telephone poles, transformers, commemorative arches, barbershops with antique furniture, tiny beauty parlours run by independent-minded lower middle class women, salons where Kollywood goes to polish up, military hotels, 'pure veg' bhavans, roadside biriyani stalls, TASMACs filled to the brim with bottles of alcohol, tools of trades, photo, video and sound studios, flex banners announcing weddings, deaths and birthdays, Xerox shops, cinema halls, Kwality Walls ice cream cycles, districts, villages, suburbs and the tunnels meant for metro rails ... all went under water.

The city's sewers filled up and the water spilt out, on to the streets, into homes, with no warning whatsoever, in the dead of the night, as darkness enveloped the city like a thick carpet. In many parts, no one heard of a flood and of officials asking them to leave to safer areas.

Officers parroted to the press that those on the banks of the Adyar should leave but there was no clarity on which areas were part of the floodplains, especially when this much water was being released. As many parts of the city were experiencing power cuts, the press statements issued by the district collector's office did not even reach the intended audience, for people were not watching TV or listening to the radio. Even if the information did reach them, many didn't realise their homes would flood. Apparently, not even the Chennai airport was prepared.

All the areas through which the Adyar winds went under. In Mudichur, the south-western suburb of Chennai, water rose to fifteen feet, destroying lives and homes. The story was just as stark in West Tambaram, Manapakkam, Meenambakkam—where, on the Adyar's floodplains, the secondary runway of the airport is located—Ekkaduthangal, Jafferkhanpet, Saidapet, Adyar, Kotturpuram, Raja Annamalaipuram and finally, the posh and upmarket MRC Nagar from where the water drains into the sea.

The Mambalam Canal, which was intended as a 'flood accommodator', and joins the Adyar, overflowed. As did the Nandanam Canal, which in turn joins the Mambalam, and further added to the woes of the people living in and around T Nagar and West Mambalam, bringing water in these areas to the height of six feet. An underground metro tunnel in Saidapet took water from the Adyar River and delivered it with great urgency to Teynampet and T Nagar, and these neighbourhoods went further under water.

On arterial roads, inside university buildings and giant IT parks, the river ran amok, its brute force threatening to knock down and carry away to the end of their lives, even the young and stable, let alone the old and frail. To walk against the current was hard and even harder to walk in its direction. Whichever way you were going, you were at risk of being pulled down by the flow, as if the river were a jealous neighbour waiting for you to fail. The only way to walk was by holding on to ropes. No one knew how to navigate this ferocious, unrecognisable being in their midst. Not the fishermen who could brave through the rough seas, nor the volunteers in sturdy jeeps and lorries, and certainly not the disaster management personnel from the armed forces.

The next day, trains, buses, share autos, cars and bikes were replaced by catamarans, coracles, fibre boats, lifeboats, large tubs, even kayaks, in which fishermen, actors, volunteers and the Good Samaritans of Chennai came out in large numbers to rescue, be rescued and in turn rescue more people.

What Caused the Floods?

A combination of factors—which occur time and again in many cities across India, particularly those on a coast—was responsible for the Chennai floods. Only a part of this was due to environmental elements beyond control such as a hot ocean possibly attributable to El Niño, high moisture content, lack of winds to carry away the clouds, and heavy rains. But the other two causes were entirely manmade: 1. Bad urban planning and 2. Abysmal disaster management planning.

The Delhi-based think tank Centre for Science and Environment captured[10] how unsustainable urban development can turn even a marginally heavy rainfall into a beast. 'Chennai had more than 600 waterbodies in the 1980s, but a master plan published in 2008 said that only a fraction of the lakes could be found in a healthy condition. The area of 19 major lakes has shrunk from a total of 1,130 hectares (ha) in the 1980s to around 645 ha in the early 2000s, reducing their storage capacity. The drains that carry surplus water from tanks to other wetlands have also been encroached upon.'

This disregard for the water ecosystem, combined with the state's utter apathy during the disaster, caused the floods in Chennai. The unpreparedness of the state was visible in shocking bureaucratic actions such as: Not opening the sluice gates of the

Chembarambakkam Reservoir days before the predicted heavy rains, which would have eased the water out through the Adyar River into the sea. Keeping the reservoir almost full despite warnings of rains. Lack of coordination between those in charge of letting water out from various reservoirs into the lakes and canals across the state. Disaster management units that were unprepared and seemingly untrained to deal with a flood and a raging river. A non-existent disaster management plan in the state. Shutting off power. Poor phone connectivity that impeded not only locating those trapped but also calling for backup by those involved in risky rescue operations. Not sending out word to people that they were about to drown.

The weather conditions did go against the city, no doubt. A parliamentary committee[11] that looked into the floods said 'that the weather in various parts of the State of Tamil Nadu changed rapidly causing deep depression between 8 November and 10 November 2015; that formed low-pressure zones over South West Bay of Bengal between 28 November and 4 December 2015. On 1 December depression struck Chennai and the adjoining districts with such great intensity that large parts of the metropolis got marooned, causing untold suffering and destruction. The devastating flood also affected the adjoining districts particularly, Cuddalore, Tiruvallur and Kancheepuram.'[12]

Despite this, the committee still blamed illegal encroachment and faulty town planning as the major cause for the floods. Long-term factors like encroachments on river plains and beds as well as lakes, stormwater drains that hadn't been desilted, lack of floodplain zone planning and large-scale settlements in low-lying areas were all held responsible. But the committee also maintained that the removal of encroachments must be a 'balanced one as it has human and social consequences.'[13] This irresponsibility of the authorities played out during the floods as well, the committee noted. The powers that be released water into the Kosasthalaiyar, the Adyar and other riverine systems, which then inundated the low-lying areas. This was further compounded when water from other lakes surrounding the city, such as Puzhal and Cholavaram, were also released.

In the course of this probe, the committee was informed by the secretary of the state's Ministry of Home Affairs that 'Obviously all state governments do take steps to prevent disasters. ... But, even if everything had been functioning absolutely perfectly, this kind of rainfall would inevitably have led to flooding. There was no way of preventing that occurrence. It happened once in 100 years.'[14]

The 'once-in-a-hundred-year-rain' theory was repeated every time someone asked questions of the state. The truth, however, is that, while it may not have rained as much in a hundred years, it almost always has been raining *like* this every decade in TN and causing floods. Moreover, a hundred-year-flood is technically not one that can happen only once in a hundred years. It simply means that in any given year, the probability of the occurrence of a flood of such high magnitude is one per cent. A hundred-year-flood can occur even in two consecutive years.[15]

The committee was unsatisfied with the government's statement, rightly, and noted in its report that 'any natural disaster of bigger intensity has the propensity to cause extensive damage. Thus, instead of putting the blame on the forces of nature, we should use advanced technology to fight it out. Moreover, the administration of both Centre and State should work together and remain vigilant to tackle the situation. [...] Natural disaster of high magnitude will always adversely affect people in large number and the administration has to respond in the fastest possible manner. Accordingly, the NDMA [National Disaster Management Authority] and all concerned bodies of central and state governments should have established procedures so that vital time is not lost in wriggling out [sic] procedural delays.'[16]

Given the repeated pattern of floods in places like Mumbai (July 2005), Surat (August 2006), Srinagar (September 2014) and then Chennai, the report said that states must scrupulously follow the NDMA guidelines and review town planning, giving importance to clearing flood passages, ensuring proper drainage, providing safe passage to excess water in lakes and other water bodies, and desiltation of river beds.

The 2005 Disaster Management Act of India, which incidentally came into force after the devastating tsunami of 2004 that ravaged coastal TN and took the lives of thousands, mandates all states to create a State Disaster Management Authority (SDMA) to oversee disaster management in every state.

The Madras High Court criticised the TN government over the defunct state of this authority. 'The Disaster Management Plan should have been dovetailed into the provisions of the ... Act long time ago and had that been done, possibly the situation which arose last year in December could have been avoided,' the judges noted in their order in 2016.[17]

Before the 2015 floods, the state's disaster management authority had met a grand total of one time, on 28 May 2013, even though a government order from 2005 requires it to meet every quarter. And during the floods, it did not meet even once.

Section 20 of the Disaster Management Act requires each state to set up a 'high power body'—a 'state executive committee' (SEC) that is responsible for implementing the plans of the SDMA, as well as, most importantly, coordinating response in the event of a disaster, like the Chennai floods.

A Comptroller and Auditor General of India (CAG) report on disaster preparedness in India in 2013 found that the SEC in TN, which was set up in January 2009, has met only once, in June 2009. There is no reference to any meetings of this SEC even during the floods. Though there was an executive council called the Tamil Nadu State Disaster Management Agency (TNSDMA), set up in January 2009, it was not the same as the one mandated in the act. The SEC, according to the act, is a statutory high power body with its membership, duties and powers all fixed by the state. The council, on the other hand, is primarily responsible for the functioning of TNSDMA. The membership, duties and powers of the mandated SEC and the executive council that was set up were entirely different. In any case, this council, whose own by-laws dictate that it meet at least once every three months, has met only five times since its inception—thrice in 2014, once in January 2015 and once in January 2016.

Given the state's track record, it is not surprising that this council too did not meet during the floods of 2015, between October and December of that year. Even more shockingly, the minutes of this council's meeting held on 13 January 2016 has no mention of the floods. Instead, the meeting seems to have dealt with nomenclature, administrative and financial issues rather than those that a high power body is supposed to be looking at in accordance with the NDMA guidelines during a crucial period.

Following the rap from the high court,[18] the State Disaster Management Plan for 2016 was eventually submitted to the court. Here is a little-known nugget: The plan was a duplication of Himachal Pradesh's plan and even had the same typographical errors. How could a hill state's disaster management plan work for Tamil Nadu? In 2018, the TN government finally came up with a State Disaster Management Perspective Plan (2018–2030) that looks at understanding and tackling disaster. It will go down as one of Chief Minister Edappadi Palaniswami's biggest legacies for he has done something that more powerful and popular chief ministers in the past have failed to do—giving the state a disaster preparedness-related goal that is also achievable. This new document proposes goals that can be accomplished by the year 2030 using systems—such as multi-hazard alert response and tracking system (like TN-SMART), real-time forecasting, spatial decision support system for major river basins and early warning systems—as well as investing in disaster management. Whether any action has been taken after the creation of this plan and whether it will continue when the next government is formed, remains to be seen. Also, can a state like TN that has been battered by natural disasters so often wait until 2030 to become truly disaster resilient, when work should have begun in earnest back in 2005?

The CAG listed out various shortcomings in the state's preparedness for the future.[19] The Centre had proposed the creation of a flood protection wall or an embankment in the Adyar River near the Nandambakkam Bridge as early as in July 2008, under its Flood Management Programme (FMG). This plan, however, was withdrawn by the chief engineer of the TN Water Resource Department in March 2012, with the state government claiming that it was not able to acquire 0.69 hectares of land for the project. The CAG felt that this could have been one of the contributing factors for heavy inundation in the Nandambakkam area of Chennai during the 2015 floods.

This report also held the state government guilty of diverting funds to works that were not approved as part of the FMG. And as the TN government delayed the submission of audited expenditure statement by up to twenty-five months, additional financial assistance promised to the state, a staggering ₹361.43 crore, was not released. The CAG also revealed that the lack of legislation for floodplain zoning in the state—marking out regions that are likely to be inundated in the event of a flood—resulted in buildings coming up along the waterways, which lead to inundation in Chennai and its suburbs during the 2015 floods.

The CAG also laid the blame on the state's Technical Advisory Committee's inertia in evicting encroachments. This committee met only twice between 2011 and 2016. Even though it had ₹400 crore at its disposal under the Twelfth Five Year Plan, the committee did not identify flood-prone areas or come up with plans to deal with floods.

In the aftermath of the flood, even as the state tried to recover from this mammoth destruction, there was a huge mismatch between the aid that the TN government requested from the Centre and what was eventually granted. The parliamentary committee that studied the floods also called for measures to address this gap.

Tamil Nadu asked for ₹25,912.45 crore towards relief and restoration work following the floods.

It received a paltry ₹1,940 crore for this 'once-in-a-hundred-year' flood.

Memories of Adyar

The Adyar River, 272 years ago, was the site of a battle that changed the course of Indian history. On its grounds, a crushing defeat was handed to Mahfuz Khan, an ally of the East India Company, by the French led by Captain Paradis, who marched with his men from Pondicherry, through Quibble Island on the Adyar Estuary, arriving at the river's southern bank. This battle seems to have happened inside both the Adyar and Cooum Rivers in Madras.

Just 500 French men had, in effect, defeated an army of 6,000 horsemen, 30,000 foot soldiers, 2,000 rocket men, 15,000 match-lock men and 30 pieces of artillery, in Mylapore near the Adyar.[20] This would then lead the British to think seriously about raising regiments of sepoys in the subcontinent, leading to further battles.

In 1870, the Adyar filled up and rose so high as to flood the barracks and parade grounds, near Palevaram (now Pallavaram), which was then eleven miles south-west of Madras. The area, about six miles from the sea, had a population of 4,000 back then (3,000 natives and 1,000 European and members of the East India Company).

A few decades later and more than a century after the Battle of Adyar, the river would no longer resemble the battleground that it was, and was very different from the polluted home of water hyacinth that it is today. In 1909, *The Theosophic Messenger: A Monthly Magazine for the Interchange of Theosophical Opinions*, published by the Theosophical Society, spoke of the kind of love the river received:[21]

> Unceasing admiration is expended on the beautiful Adyar river, which divides the property of the Theosophical Society from Adyar proper—a suburb five miles to the south of Madras, and after crossing the elegant bridge of seventeen arches very near the Theosophical Headquarters, a feeling of contentment tempts the wish never to cross back again into the world that knows not the complete satisfaction of life in this little paradise. Following the river along for about a mile and a half through the grounds of the Society, brings one to the Bay of Bengal, the eastern boundary which improves the picturesqueness and temperature very much. In these waters the early riser catches glimpses of the most wondrous reflections and combinations of colours, principally gold, so gloriously brilliant and variable with each new day. The Sunset is equally magnificent and its radiance over the water through the great variety of green trees, plants and flowers, cause the residents to seek the many views, all as beautiful as they are diverse.

If you were out and about at sunset a few years later, in 1921, you might have run into an officer who too seems to have loved the river dearly. From the anonymous accounts of his time in India, we learn that some things have just not changed in Madras. Like, 'you do not have to dress terrifically'[22] while you are in this city. We do loathe sartorial despotism.[23] And that one of the most delightful things about Madras is that it is at the edge of India from where the 'blue Bay rolls in at its feet'.[24] The writer waxed eloquent on the Adyar and its sanguine sunsets: [25]

> In Madras, too, the Civilian discovered a great river called the Adyar, on the banks of which stands a Club that looks exactly like a piece of the old White City of Shepherd's Bush. Perhaps it is. On the Adyar you may for a consideration row in boats. The Civilian cannot row, and frequently incommoded his fellow athletes, but he liked the Adyar. It is chiefly notable for kingfishers and sunsets; there are three different kinds of kingfisher and a different sunset every night. The kingfishers sit upon a telegraph wire which crosses the river and make suicidal plunges at intervals; two sorts of them "a large and a small" are red and blue just like our own at home, and the third and most delightful is black and white. The sunsets on the Adyar are the most wonderful things, for they always come on after the sun is out of sight. He goes down away up the river behind a bank of cloud and everything becomes chilly and dull; the false sunset in the East dies out and there falls a tremendous silence. You are to wait a quarter of an hour or so and then you must say, "There will be no sunset to-night." This breaks the spell and suddenly you feel the faintest of breezes at your cheek and a wave of orange light leaps up from all sides at once, glowing and swelling and deepening into purest rose. It will last perhaps a quarter of an hour, and for that quarter of an hour you may drift in an enchanted world of colours the banks and the water and the kingfishers and even your own dull and prosaic self all charmed into a new and rose-coloured existence. At the end of this time the spell will flit as suddenly as it came and the world will settle down to a quiet silver grey in the hope of a moon to come. Now there are sunsets and sunsets, but this sort of thing does not happen except on the

> Adyar. Sunrise in India is good almost everywhere, but for these reasons the Civilian thinks you must go to the Adyar to see the sun setting.

Fair warning, the Civilian's love seems to have run dry when it comes to the 'indigenous' people of Madras. In this very book, there are pages upon pages detailing the exact kind of contempt the colonisers had for the colonised. In his bid to prove to the English audience that the 'funny native' trope of the locals is false and that actually they are dangerous, he writes, 'The Indian servant, peon, coolie, artisan, tradesman, or lower-class subordinate is not really funny ...'[26] and that British civilians like him '... live among a people whose aim and intention is to cheat you, to defraud you, to bewilder and bamboozle you, to exploit you for every anna, every half-anna, every pice and pie you are worth.'[27] Among many other offensive things, he also writes, '... your dressing-boy wears your shirt and gives you eczema—if nothing worse.'[28] Several anecdotes dehumanise the people who served him and these stories have titles such as 'Fable of the Lagging Coolie', 'The Implacable Kshatriyas', and 'The Sweeper's Cow'.

In 1928, Allister Macmillan, in his book *Seaports of India & Ceylon,* described the many 'delightful' sites built around the Adyar:[29]

> The Adyar Club commands a delightful prospect over the River Adyar, while close by is the Madras Boat Club. Just outside the Municipal toll gate is the Elphinstone Bridge across the Adyar. On the opposite side of the river is the handsomely laid out compound of the Theosophical Society, when Mrs Annie Besant introduced to the world the Indian youth, Krishnamurti, as the embodiment of the new Messiah for the redemption of humanity.

But not much later, in 1939, things were not so different from 2018, it would appear. Percy Macqueen, the then district collector of Nilgiris, wrote in the *Madras Tercentenary Commemoration Volume*.[30]

> During recent years the north bank of Adyar has been rapidly developing into a teeming suburb. It was formerly a quiet resort of the wealthy Europeans, who lived in a few large mansions surrounded by wide lawns and big trees which recalled the features of an English Park. The mansions still remain but the parks are rapidly disappearing under a load of bricks and mortar.

Soon after, in October 1943, Madras drowned. On the same day, it also came under its only air attack from a Japanese aircraft in the Second World War.[31] There were no military damages but there were a few civilian casualties, newspapers reported. The bomb did not take many lives but the flood did. The Cooum and the Adyar flooded, inundating nearly half of the city, though the damage from the Cooum was far worse than from the Adyar in those floods. In an interview to *The Hindu,* recalling the 1943 floods, naturalist V. Guruswami said:[32]

> It was a holiday and we—my brother Kalyanasundaram, our cousin Swaminathan and I—decided to spend the day at the house of our brother-in-law at the Egmore Railway Quarters. We left Triplicane and reached Egmore around 9 a.m. It was raining heavily, but we had no idea that in the evening, we would trudge back home in waters that would threaten to swallow us. As the flood waters rose dramatically, residents of the quarters abandoned their houses and took shelter in the wagons stationed in the Railway yard. There was no let-up in the rain and we decided to brave it out and return home on

> foot. It turned out to be a hare-brained decision, because the Gandhi–Irwin Road was under water that was waist-high for a tall adult. Whenever a heavy motor vehicle trundled past, the waters would rush in waves towards us.

People were washed away or died as their homes crumbled on them, boats plied the roads of Madras, dead cattle were seen drifting away, and the river banks carried an extraordinary amount of furniture that had been washed away from people's homes. Older parts of the city like Mylapore, George Town, Royapuram and Triplicane miraculously did not flood.[33] And this would repeat itself in 2015.

Love and Loss on the Banks of the Adyar

On the morning of the floods, the family of Anantha Narayanan, who live in the southern suburb of Keezhkattalai, asked Narayanan to not go to work because of the rain forecast. His workplace abuts the Maraimalai Adigalar Bridge—the first to be constructed on the Adyar upon an olden causeway by the Armenian trader Coja Petrus Uscan in 1726, and which would later that day be submerged, cutting off access to large chunks of the city.

It was a Tuesday, and every Tuesday evening there was a face-to-face meeting of the entire team; Narayanan was not going to skip it. He took an early morning train to work, instead of his bike. Through the entire journey, he kept tabs on the rains through Facebook. He assumed that trains weren't going to stop, and he could always go back home should things get bad. There would definitely at least be an autorickshaw out there that would take him home from the station, if not an Uber or Ola. Even though his own home was just a hundred metres away from the Keezhkattalai Lake, and his office was on the banks of the Adyar, he was not worried. At all. He didn't have an inkling of what lay ahead.

'The next time something like this happens, I will think twice about venturing out. But at that time, there was no history. So I never thought it would happen,' he said, when I met him months later.

It was a work day like any other, except he was fully drenched despite having travelled by train and keeping his raincoat on. Narayanan had a spare shirt, thankfully. It was a cold day in the office, with the air conditioning on. At 5.30 in the evening, the meeting started as always, and by 6 he was thinking of leaving. That's when he heard from colleagues that trains were being stopped near the Pallavaram area because railway tracks were blocked by water. Pallavaram is a historical neighbourhood in Chennai where a hand axe belonging to the Lower Palaeolithic Age was discovered for the first time in the entire subcontinent, before a wide array of such discoveries were made elsewhere.[34] It proved that the environs of Chennai were inhabited during the Stone Age. It was also a cantonment under the Mughals and later the British. Archival maps from the British period show that the Adyar heavily inundated Pallavaram as early as 1827 and 1870.

Narayanan decided to take the train till Pallavaram that day and head home from there. He took a different street to the station and not the one he usually used because he was warned by those on the street that there was water up to the waist there.

~

At the Annai Special School in VGP Salai that is just a little away from Narayanan's office, on the river's banks, K.S. Mariappan was stuck alone with four of his pupils, all with mental disabilities. Mariappan, who uses crutches as a result of a polio attack, would later that night wade through chest-high water, and with the help of local autorickshaw drivers, transport the students to a colleague's home. Mariappan would himself have to be carried upon the shoulders of bystanders to safety, as would the kids.[35] Not even V.G. Santhosam, the current chairman of the VGP group and the brother of V.G. Panneer Das—after whom the road is named—would be spared. He would see eleven feet of water enter his home in Saidapet, and would leave with his family, on a boat. He would remember the floods of 1985, when he was on a boat himself rescuing and helping others, and smirk at fate.[36]

Worried about their very futures, just a few hundred metres away from both Narayanan and Mariappan, were the inhabitants of Thideer Nagar in Saidapet. Thideer, meaning sudden, is the name given to areas of settlements of huts in Chennai. As these hutments pop up overnight, the area they are located in is called Thideer Nagar—Sudden Settlement. Chennai has many such Thideer Nagars. The Thideer Nagar in Saidapet has two 'batches' of settlers. The older ones who have been resettled there by the government in concrete homes and the newer ones who live in thatched-roof huts.

In just a few hours, the horror of it all would sink in. Even as Thideer Nagar's 1,000 families stayed huddled in nearby schools, the Adyar would swallow whole thatched huts made of thousands of woven coconut fronds that cost each of its poor owners nearly ₹10,000, and a few hundred kilos of casuarina poles that cost at least ₹5,000 per home. And when it's done with its holy mess, the river would leave nothing behind. Not even a trace of where their homes once stood. At the older Thideer Nagar, with its concrete walls and tin roofs, the shell would stand, hollowed out, while everything inside would have drifted away,[37] like a tiny plant caught in the path of an elephant running amok, as the angry river would go on a rampage reclaiming its path.

What Thideer Nagar residents did not know then was also that in less than two years, the entire lot of them would lose access to the city, as they would be relocated far outside the metropolis as a consequence of what happened that day.

Further up ahead from Thideer Nagar, the 150 families who call Salavayalar Colony their home would watch as Dhobi Khana in West Saidapet, where the Saidapet Salavayalar Sangam or the Washer People's Union office is, goes under. In a few hours, the waters would devour everything here too, and the inhabitants of the area, resettled here by the late chief minister Kamaraj, would have to leave their homes and workplace, not walking, but swimming and atop boats, bundling up what they could. They would watch as the Adyar takes away with it all that they had saved up through a lifetime of hard work of beating, washing, steaming and ironing clothes. Among the things the river would take with it would be precious trousseau gathered for the wedding of a young woman, scheduled to take place in less than a week, even as her father Irudhayaraj would watch helplessly, reduced to tears.[38]

~

Narayanan caught a train at around 6.30 p.m., along with a friend who decided to leave his car behind in the office. To reach the next station, Guindy, the train took fifteen minutes, as opposed to the usual five. They were beginning to get restless about the train's speed when they realised that every time another train passed them, theirs had to stop. The tracks were all flooded. To reach the railway station near the Chennai airport, which was en route to Narayanan's home and only around six kilometres away, it took them two hours. In the train, Narayanan met students of IIT Madras with huge suitcases, on their way out of town, like the several thousand that were looking to flee it. The students told him that they couldn't flag down an autorickshaw and had to walk five kilometres with their luggage to the Guindy station.

What the students of IIT Madras didn't know just then was that at 8.30 p.m., the airport would officially stop operations and close to 5,000 people inside would be stranded—some on transit, others to see off a loved one and many on their way out to other cities.

Without paying heed to warnings from environmentalists and aviation experts, the 2,925-metre secondary runway of the Chennai airport was built on the flood basin of the Adyar in 2011, by erecting a bridge over it and hindering its path. As early as 2008, aviation safety specialists such as Captain Ranganathan had expressed apprehensions over this very possibility, calling this endeavour a 'white elephant'.[39] Predictions were made. And they would come true, stopping those IIT students and others from escaping a flooding city. The prophecies included warnings of the Chembarambakkam Reservoir overflowing into the Adyar, and the river's flow being constrained by this secondary runway, causing extensive flooding in the surrounding areas. As always, these warnings fell on indifferent ears.

Just as foretold, here was the Adyar, to claim its right of way.

Their flights too cancelled, husband Maruthanayagam and wife Nirmala Pushpam, the vice principal of a city school, would hail a cab later on, and try to go home to Pallikaranai's

IIT Colony. The taxi driver would drop them off at Velachery about five kilometres from the couple's home, beyond which he would tell them it was impossible for his car to go. There would be too much water. Unaware of a breach in the nearby Kovilambakkam Lake, the couple would try to walk home. Their bodies would be found five days later, in a pile, washed away by the lake, along with eight others. The couple would leave behind their grieving mothers and a ten-year-old son and a seven-year-old daughter.[40]

Narayanan and his friend reached Pallavaram that was two stations away from his home at 11.45 p.m. Only one platform was operational at the Pallavaram station that night. So all the trains had to go past the station, change tracks and come back to the sole working platform. At one point, Narayanan saw six electric trains, in a row, like ducks in a pond.

He was not big on carrying a lot of cash—even before demonetisation—and had just about ₹200 in hand. No ATM nearby was working. It was pitch dark outside the Pallavaram station. The two of them walked to GST Road, about a kilometre away, which still had cars and trucks plying. Most restaurants had shut and the ones that were open wanted cash. So the two of them didn't eat. His friend decided to go back to the station and spend the night there. Narayanan asked him to come home, which was a mere three kilometres from where they were. His friend didn't want to get stuck in Narayanan's house and so went his way. Narayanan tried to flag down vehicles late in the night, but no one stopped. About half-a-kilometre later, as he was turning into the 200 Feet Road, a car stopped to ask him if the road was open.

'I think it is, because I have been seeing cars and bikes go and come', Narayanan said.

'All the subways between here and Pallikaranai are flooded and closed. I need to go home to Pallikaranai. Do you think I can?' the driver asked him. Narayanan made a guesstimate and said that this was a wide four-lane highway and that he didn't think there was going to be any flooding here, so the man could possibly go all the way to Pallikaranai. The car's owner had gone to the airport at 11.30 that morning to board a flight. He had, in fact, been sitting inside a flight ready to take off, but was then told the airport was closing, and sent back.

Narayanan finally got a lift from the man. By then it was 12.15 in the night. They drove on, but a kilometre before Narayanan's home, the car was stopped. The road was closed and a rope had been tied across it. It looked like people had been there for hours, because in many of the cars parked there, the headlights were off and people were fast asleep inside.

He could see his apartment building and told the policeman in charge that he wanted to head home, pointing to it. He was allowed to go. As he walked on the highway that was built across a lake, he heard water flowing furiously. Usually, at this part of the road, there was no sound of water because it was all just still water. By the time he reached his building, there was water up to his waist.

Right outside his building was an old canal—it usually just had sewage water flowing through it. That night, it was sewage and more. Before he could figure out what was going on, he was staring at six feet of water in front of his building. When he finally battled the water and stepped inside his home, it was 12.30 a.m.

Upon reaching home, Narayanan would realise that Meera and his mother-in-law had been through a dreadful couple of hours waiting for him and his sister-in-law, Lavanya.

~

Lavanya was coming back home in an office bus from Sholinganallur, on the IT corridor of the city, and was dropped off at the Keezhkattalai bus stand, after a lot of confusion and traffic at around 5.45 in the evening. Lavanya had seen the lakes breaching the 200 Feet Road en route and water spreading everywhere.

It was chaos when she got off the bus—backed up traffic, flooded roads and what not, and she was just about wondering how to get to her sister's home a mere 250 metres away. As she waded in slowly through the water, there was fear of being electrocuted or falling into a manhole. The water was dangerously high in many smaller roads. It had become dark and there was no power.

That is when she ran into two acquaintances who lived close by. She decided to walk with them. Halfway through, they were again standing in waist-deep water. It was as if they were walking through a river. Were they? The three held hands and reached an apartment building that was built at a higher level, and waited in the parking lot. Four 'bachelors' who were living in that building in a 3 BHK flat on the second floor offered their home to this rain-washed trio.

They stayed the night in the strangers' flat. The next morning, the three of them waded through chest-level water and reached one of their homes. From that building's rooftop terrace, Narayanan and his family could see Lavanya and she could see them, and they waved to each other. They couldn't do much else.

Finally, later in the day, the Pallavaram municipality brought a boat to rescue people. The boat went in, brought Lavanya out and took her home.

Even as more rains were being forecast and people were being asked to leave, through announcements on megaphones, nobody was leaving. The Pallavaram municipality chairman visited and said, 'We are here trying to save people but they don't even want to leave their homes. Tomorrow if something happens to them, the blame will fall squarely on us and they'll say we didn't do anything.'

Until Narayanan reached, there was confusion at home. Until they heard from Lavanya, there was more of it. But once the family was united, all was well because they had power backup. So from the air conditioning to the internet, everything was working fine.

The rest of the city wasn't as lucky.

Washed Out by the River

> The banks of the little river Adyar presented a curious spectacle for all the washing of the capital was being done there by a thousand dhobies, male and female, near the bridge; and the river-sands were covered with countless garments of all colours, while the air was filled with the thunder of a thousand wet cloths slapped upon the flat stones.

From Edwin Arnold's observations in *India Revisited,*[41] two things are clear: that a thousand men and women worked on the banks of the Adyar washing clothes, and that travellers visited Marmalong Bridge to watch them, as also attested by other traveller accounts from that period. They also took pictures and made postcards of these people. This continues to this day, for no dhobi ghat or dhobi khana in India is without camerapersons wielding bulky DSLRs and taking pictures of those hard at work, with or without consent, participating in a gaze that fetishises caste-based labour.

~

Banu Chandran was born in Salavayalar Colony, and first lived in Gotha Medu or Kotha Medu, in this colony, on the banks of the Adyar in Saidapet. After she finished class five, she moved to Satya Nagar, also on the banks of this river, to take care of her brother's baby, and then to the nearby Rangarajapuram after her marriage. She has lived around this one river her entire life, which at most times is just about snaking through the city with just a little 'water'. Chandran's current home is located behind Srinagar Colony where my parents live, near Little Mount—legend has it that one of the twelve apostles of Jesus Christ, St Thomas, lived and was martyred here.

We residents seldom remember that all four of these places—Little Mount, Srinagar Colony, Satya Nagar and Rangarajapuram—are on the banks of the Adyar, even though, every day, we cross the Marmalong alias Maraimalai Adigal alias Saidapet Bridge, which connects South Chennai to the older parts of the city.

'My parents were also salavai thozhilali,' Chandran said, when I met her after the floods. Salavai means washer and thozhilali means worker. 'My father ironed clothes until very late in his life, and my mother helped him. They didn't want to rely on anyone even in their old age. They earned their own wages until the end. They wouldn't even come to my house; they were very independent.'

Chandran's current home in Rangarajapuram is an independent, one-storeyed, tiled-roof building. Over the last two decades, the occupants of Rangarajapuram have seen the prices of their property grow higher, and prosperity has been ushered in. Many have sold their lands, and apartment buildings have replaced old homes, while others have remodelled and built multi-storeyed homes that perk up the narrow roads with their dazzling vastu colours—here an orange or there a purple.

There's a small room on the ground floor in Chandran's house, which is now occupied by tenants; it wasn't on the night the river breached. Chandran lives on the first floor. Since she's closer to the roof, she endures the harsh sun between the months of March and June. It is this hot home, on the first floor, that would save a vast amount of her life's belongings from being washed away in the floods.

This area has never flooded as badly as it did in December, according to Chandran. 'There would be water and flooding every Diwali, back when I lived in Satya Nagar,' she recalled. But the only time they had to move out of their home and into the Anna University campus, which is on the other side of the Adyar across Satya Nagar, was in 2005, during the floods that took the lives of over 150 people from across the state. That year, water lurked around their ground-floor room, but seemed to change its mind and go away quietly, winding down a different path. Some years later, it came almost up to the entrance of their home, but then drained away.

'This is the third flood I am witnessing since moving to this area. And this is the biggest one of them all. This time, not only did the river submerge our ground floor entirely but also came up to the staircase leading to our home in the first floor. No one came to tell us to go anywhere and there wasn't even very heavy rain that day here. So we didn't expect it to flood like that. We didn't go anywhere because we didn't think there was any reason to. Two whole days later, we see them coming in boats,' she said, with annoyance and resignation. 'And they ask us, forty-eight horrible hours later, if we want soru [rice]; if we want thanni [water].'

If she had been warned, Chandran said, she would have emptied out the ground-floor room, gone somewhere safer or at least bought rations. 'Until the end, everyone in the area was convinced that it wouldn't come into our homes. We all thought, just as before, the water would tease us and threaten us, but in the end it won't take us out.' Take them out, it did. For three days, the entire family was stuck upstairs, cooped up in the room on the first floor. Without water and access to even a bathroom, which was also submerged, they managed by cooking whatever was in the house. They ate goduma ravai (wheat semolina) and ration shop pacha arisi kanji (raw rice porridge).

Besides all the things that were in the ground-floor room, Chandran also lost an old potti—a brass iron box with wooden handle—which works on hot coal and is way more expensive than the electric ones and had been in the family for years. 'My husband left it below because we needed to get it repaired. It's gone now,' she said. Chandran's family is finally picking up the pieces after the floods and is moving on, three years later.

~

In Satya Nagar live some of the oldest occupants of this neighbourhood, having been here for over forty years. It is their tin-roofed, concrete shell homes that are affected first, whenever there is a downpour, and it is they, the original inhabitants of this erstwhile forest-like landscape, that bear the brunt of evictions when the city wants to 'beautify' its rivers and banks. While many of the old residents have moved out, renting out their homes to live elsewhere and do other jobs that promise a better life, a few remain here because they work close by. Some of the older women from this neighbourhood work in universities as peons or as household help and nannies, while the older men work as autorickshaw drivers, sell plastic wares in exchange for old clothes, and so on. These homes have borne witness to struggles of people from the working class and the oppressed castes, who have strived to give their children quality education, and who are all now slowly beginning to see the dividends of education. The older women and men have finally stopped working so hard, because their children, who now work in companies in the city, earn handsomely. These dividends are a result of their proximity to the city, its educational institutions and that river that wrecks their home as it pleases. This advantage of proximity received a fatal blow in December 2015.

Even though there was no warning, the people of Satya Nagar, seeing a swollen Adyar, left their homes and sought shelter in the nearby schools, twice—once in November and then in December. Even though they had been dry and safe elsewhere during the December floods, they came back home to huge mounds of sludge, mud from the banks and all the waste that the river had carried in, and smeared their homes with, from the ground up to the roof. It took the inhabitants of this area, who live a mere few metres away from the river, months to clean up their home, and several people I spoke to said they received the maximum aid from volunteers and very little from the State.

Now Satya Nagar is nearly empty. Many of its residents have moved into homes allotted to them in Semmenchery, twenty-six kilometres away, as part of the large eviction drive after the floods displaced the people living along the Adyar and Cooum. Some are still around for various reasons—their work is close by and they don't want to move to the middle of nowhere or they haven't been allotted a home and allege that local politicians demand a bribe of up to ₹40,000 for the allotment of a single housing unit. Some want to leave because they no longer wish to live in this 'seru and sagathi' or mud and waste, some don't want to leave because this is the only place they know. The demolition drive is yet to begin and its threat looms large.

An Invisible People

If there were ever apprehensions about the Indian news media and its attitude to places outside of Delhi and Mumbai, they were all dispelled during the floods of 2015. All through November, as the suburbs of Chennai and the villages in TN flooded and the city was in the throes of a disaster, the national media ignored the news. Not many from the city called the media out then, because Chennai, like many other parts of this vast country that are ignored by its media, was used to it. In fact, nobody even expected the national media to report on issues pertaining to the city with any nuance. But something tipped that December. Even as the city turned into an island and was plunged into deep darkness, as lives were being lost and a disaster of unimaginable proportions was underway, there was not a squeak in the national media about it. For those who were marooned, it didn't make any difference, but for those outside, the silence was deafening and demeaning. The country's first city, it's fourth largest metropolis, with close to seventy-one lakh people had become invisible. There was no information about an entire city even as those outside the flood-affected areas waited helplessly, unable to find out just what had happened to their loved ones.

If there was news anywhere, it was only on social media. From rain forecasts to rescue coordination, the city depended on volunteers sitting as far away as Bengaluru or even the USA, and the hundreds and thousands in Chennai's few dry areas with power or internet. Many victims of the floods who had managed to get to safer, drier places, found themselves shaken from whatever lull they had been experiencing. It was a wakeup call, being this close to disaster and realising that help was not forthcoming, from anywhere. So they began volunteering to help the others still in trouble.

The state knew about the kind of rains that were to batter the city and its suburbs. Why this never translated into action is anybody's guess, as officials have maintained that they did all they could but it was the 'once-in-a-hundred-year-rains' that was responsible for the floods.

For information on rains during those crucial days, and ever since, Chennai hasn't had to look too far. A handful of pluviophiles, hobbyists posting on weather blogs, have since become our go-to guys. The most reliable among them, known to us as TamilNadu Weatherman, is Pradeep John.[42] John was right and the BBC's weather predictions wrong, more than once that December. With all of 1000 likes on his Facebook page till then, he went on to capture the city's heart with his forecasting in November 2015. Today, there are over 50,000 reviews on his page and over 6 lakh likes and almost everyone in the state recognises him, thanks to the regional media that has rightly showered him with accolades and admiration. John has been blogging about rains since 2010 and has been interested in them from when he was fourteen years old.

As early as 8 November, John wrote on his Facebook page, 'Depression causes havoc as highest rains of the year lash Chennai and surrounding regions ... Massive inflow can be expected in

Redhills Lake tomorrow.' He followed this up on 19 November with, 'These easterlies are difficult to predict w.r.t. intensity with sudden inflow of moisture, they can dump heavy rains in short period. Avadi which is already suffering from floods was badly hit by today evening rains. Chennai city got just 3 mm....'

By 23 November, his updates contained even more prophetic statements, such as: '... the worst news—more rains to follow. Particularly in the worst hit flood areas of south Chennai and ECR. Chennai has crossed 1000 mm for the month of November in 2015. Only in 2005 October and 1918 November we have got more rains. Soon it will break those two months and will be wettest month ever.'

As early as 28 November, he had written about the convergence and divergence that we would read about in the news only after the floods. 'What is this actually, is it a depression or cyclone? ... Divergence and Convergence is increasing and it's going to be night time the strongest period for NEM'. B. Mukhopadhyay, Additional Director–General of Meteorology (research), India Meteorological Department (IMD), Pune, told *The Hindu,*[43] 'An individual episode like that on 1 December is a combination of several factors and in every such episode, the combination changes. On 1 December, the lower-level moisture supply was high and upper air evacuation of the moisture was also strong. We call this phenomenon upper air divergence, and the effect is that the cloud becomes very intense. Both coincide very rarely.'

Even though there were warnings for rains from the IMD, the sun was out and about even as late as 29 November. This led several people into clutching at a false sense of hope that the predictions were wrong. John, though, was insistent. 'There has been a weird delay in rains lashing in Chennai, but models still continue to show unrelenting rains from today till next 3 days. This may be the 1st time in so many years when both the models predicted rains and have failed in their predictions.'

And then he wrote, later on the same day: '... we are expecting some activity from tonight or tomorrow into next 3–4 days. The meteogram for Chennai show large continuous rains. It's only indicative tool but confirms chance of heavy rains. As I told earlier, one day of the next few days will get that heavy flooding type rains.'

He was right, of course.

A Tamil documentary on Cyclone Ockhi—which took the lives of several hundred fisherfolk from TN and Kerala in November 2017—by Divya Bharathi, asked why a country with sophisticated technology was unable to predict and warn people ahead of calamities, when a hobbyist like John could. FIRs were promptly filed against Bharati just four days after she released the trailer for *Orutharum Varela* (*Nobody Came*) on 28 June 2018 on the grounds that her film 'insulted the national flag, promoted disharmony between communities, disturbed public tranquillity and portrayed the government in bad light'. And then came news of intimidations from the local police and even threats to her safety.

Why, indeed, was the state unable to reach out to people even as weather bloggers like John did?

#ChennaiRains

With the birth of a hashtag, #ChennaiRains, a new way to deal with the crisis was born. At least, initially, and for those of us with tech skills. Volunteers in safer places were looking up tweets under this hashtag and attending to people's needs—checking in on someone's parents, calling people up, connecting those stuck with rescue workers, aid and more. As local celebrities like actor Siddharth—who said he 'freaked out' that he had lost his house, three studios and three cars for the first time—lent their support, the hashtag gained a lot of momentum. With the help of a more egalitarian medium, radio, and celebrity RJs like Balaji throwing their weight behind it, the social media support spilt over on to the streets.

Massive spontaneous rescue teams were formed across the city. People hired large vehicles to recce flood-hit areas and rescued those stranded, and hundreds reached out with essential supplies. Trucks filled with food, water and more were coming in from states near and far.

The Jain temple on GN Chetty road churned out 5,000 packets of breakfast, lunch and dinner. All mosques in the city opened up their doors for people irrespective of their faiths. Major cinema halls like Sathyam and Mayajaal also opened their gates to those stranded. Strangers opened up their homes.

Restaurants like the Old Madras Baking Company and Double Roti offered food and a resting place for free to those who were passing by, while Jonah's and Tryst Cafe delivered it straight to those in need. You could rest assured that if someone in the city was not affected by the floods or had escaped it after being stuck briefly, they were involved in rescue and relief work during those four days in Chennai. The city organised itself in an admirable manner and even in the midst of all that heartbreak, there was something heartwarming happening somewhere in the city.

Like when the young engineer and volunteer, Muhammed Yunus, after hearing about the 800-odd people stuck in Urappakkam, found seven boatmen willing to brave the waters and go on a rescue mission. Chitra, who was pregnant and due in two days, and her spouse Mohan were among those who needed to be rescued. Yunus, along with the boatmen, helped the couple reach safety, from where they made it to a hospital in Perungalathur. Chitra delivered a baby girl and named her Yunus.[44]

Not all help during these floods, however, was ad-hoc. Some, armed with the experience of having worked during several disasters, stepped in, and soon, an assembly-line-like system was set up. Bhoomika Trust, which works in the areas of disaster relief and rehabilitation, networked with many other NGOs and organised one of the largest relief centres in the city.

Bhoomika set up a control room to rerout messages and calls of distress to concerned authorities and teams in the respective zones. A massive community kitchen began operations on 3 December and distributed an average of 30,000 to 40,000 food packages a day through different groups of volunteers and NGOs.

'The community kitchen predominantly coordinated with volunteers and citizens of Chennai. Between 3 December and 9 December, Bhoomika distributed 1,90,000 food packages,' Latha Subramaniam of the trust said. The large community kitchen and the disaster relief kit packing section had over 10,000 volunteers clocking more than 1 lakh volunteer-hours in all. For 70,000 families going back home after the floods, Bhoomika offered dry ration kits with rice, dal, oil, tamarind and spices for fifteen days. The trust has also been involved in long-term rehabilitation of victims from remote villages and continues to help them with housing.

In the week after the flood, my aunt, who works in a school for Adi Dravida children, told me over the phone that many families near her village outside Chennai had lost everything, and that 'her kids'—as she likes to call her students—didn't have as much as clothes. I was able to quickly source dry rations through Bhoomika for over a hundred families, and what I witnessed when I went to their relief camp was terrific and impressive. Bhoomika was operating out of a large wedding hall, where I saw hundreds and thousands of people walking in and out with aid. I had no connections to the trust. When I reached there, I called a friend who was volunteering. The next thing I knew, my aunt was sitting in the front seat of a mini-truck we booked using Lynk, an Uber-like app for trucks, with the dry ration kits. She was also carrying clothes for her students, which I had picked up from my friend Amba's home, who was also helping out those affected. I had told her about the clothing needs of school children of various ages over Facebook messenger and Telegram. As phone services were largely disrupted, relief work in the days following the floods was organised over social media and WhatsApp.

My appreciation for my smartphone and the interwebs grew manifold that day. But this also highlighted how the divide between those who had access to resources and those who did not was reflected in the digital world as well. This stark digital divide stood out during the floods, alongside the fact that the marginalised across the state were unable to access relief, even though others could claim it easily. It was not for lack of trying. There were forces at play that were working hard to deny some people aid, while ensuring that others got it.

Pianist Anil Srinivasan was involved in rescue, relief as well as rehabilitation of flood victims in the city. During the floods, he worked with the National Disaster Response Force (NDRF) over the phone, directing them to people who needed to be rescued. Eighteen other volunteers camped at his third-floor apartment and helped with the coordination. Once rescue work ended, he joined an initiative by the Rotary Club of Madras, of which he is a member, to put together a relief centre.

The Hyatt hotel opened up its storage space as a relief camp as well as provided meals for all the volunteers. Srinivasan, along with Ashok Thakkar of Rotary, wanted to do more. The then commissioner of Chennai Corporation, Vikram Kapoor, told them that children displaced after the floods from the Adyar's banks to Perumbakkam, an area seventeen kilometres away from their earlier home, needed a school.

Srinivasan donated his entire earnings from 2016 to the school. Vish Vishwanathan of Anuja San Antonio, 'a non-profit created to promote sister-city alliance between San Antonio [Texas, USA] and Chennai' too offered support. With the help of doctors in San Antonio, many of whom are from Chennai, and with the help of other NGOs, Vishwanathan managed to raise

$200,000. The Tata group's CSR initiative donated the remaining funds, ₹3.9 crore, to complete the school. 'It took us until the end of 2016 to raise the funds, ₹5 crore,' Srinivasan said, 'The Corporation of Madras has given us the land. Running around to get permissions took us another six months. The school is now coming up really well. We have a large library space.' This consortium of do-gooders will handover the school for the children of Perumbakkam to the city corporation by June 2019.

The flood has come and gone but the rehabilitation process of those affected continues to this day in Chennai and elsewhere in the state.

'It Was the Worst Day of My Life'

Dr Bala Kumari's KS Hospital is in Velachery, an area in South Chennai that has grown exponentially over the last twenty years. Born in Melnedumbur, a village near Chidambaram district, Dr Bala was the first girl in her family to have studied beyond class five, and back then, even the men in her family had studied only up to class twelve. It was her father who identified a spark in her as early as when she was in class two. 'He figured I was studious and decided to educate me,' Dr Bala said, when I met her one overcast day in her hospital. There was opposition from the relatives, who had a lot to say to her father: 'Why are you educating a girl?' and 'After getting married she'll only be supporting her husband's family and not you.' Her father had only one retort: 'If my daughter is happy and fulfilled in her life that is enough for me, I don't expect anything from her.' This drove Dr Bala to work hard. 'I wanted to give back to society, to my village and to my family, and I have strived to not deviate from this goal.' She named her hospital after her father—KS stands for Kanaka Sabapathy.

A leading gynaecologist and obstetrician in Chennai today, Dr Bala had been practising in the heart of Chennai, Teynampet, for nearly thirty years, at an outpatient clinic, admitting her patients at a nursing home nearby when needed. In 2000, she decided to start a hospital, or 'a small set-up' as she calls it.

'Neither I nor my husband come from financially sound backgrounds,' she said. Teynampet's real estate was expensive, so she decided to look for a place in the periphery of the city. It also had to be less than thirty minutes away from her old workplace because she had to continue to work there in order to support her family and fund the new venture. 'I also wanted it to be a place where there was a need for my work,' she said. She combed the city for over a year and finally found a place in Velachery through a friend.

'If I want to do a project like this now, I won't be able to.' Land value in these parts has increased fifteen times since, Dr Bala told me. But even in Velachery, she had to pick a location away from the main road—where land was still unaffordable—and zeroed in on a spot that was surrounded by shrubbery and a smattering of houses here and there. There were no other hospitals in the area, and it seemed like the perfect spot.

'It was tough, but it was my dream,' she said. 'Once you have your own set-up, you can cater to anybody. The rich and the poor. I don't claim to do free service but, in my hospital, I have control over the charges. If I want to help somebody, I can do it without a worry. I don't have to ask someone else.'

In 2005, five years after Dr Bala bought the land, the hospital started functioning with an initial staff of six. The first year, the hospital performed a hundred deliveries. Today, the hospital has six more gynaecologists, one general doctor, two anaesthetists and two paediatricians. The hospital saw 826 deliveries in 2017 and 714 in 2018.

Dr Bala was also keen on helping young women back in her village. 'There's this school in my village. I went there and asked what girls do after class twelve. There wasn't much work coming by. I asked some of them if they would like to come and do nursing here. These were people working in the paddy fields, after their twelfth. They said they would.' Dr Bala began conducting nursing courses in the hospital, and for the next two to three years, there was a regular stream of young women from her village. 'These days, they go in for software courses. But some of them are still here, working, while some have left after marriage.'

During the first monsoon after construction work on the hospital had started, Dr Bala saw lotuses blooming in the ground next to her plot. That is when she realised that she had been sold a piece of land where a lake had once stood. 'People say, "You were the one who went and built on a lake." But we don't. The government sells this land. Who gave permission to the government to do this? There was no way for us to know what this was. I felt really bad, and whenever it rained, this entire area was surrounded by water and there were lotuses and lilies everywhere. But we had already bought this place and started building. So we couldn't do anything.'

In the second year of its operation, the hospital was marooned. At that time, there were only two patients and they had already delivered. They were moved out in a boat for about 500 metres and then sent to other hospitals for postnatal care.

Since then, there had been no major flooding in the hospital. Until 2015. That year, the hospital flooded thrice. While there were two rounds of flooding across the city—on 17 November and the more disastrous one on 1 December—parts of the city that regularly flood every monsoon, including Velachery where Dr Bala's hospital is, experienced inundation twice in November. 'The first time, there was warning and we stopped admissions. There was an inch of water inside the hospital during the first floods.' Once the water came in, everything, including the sump, became unsterile. The entire hospital was washed and disinfected and the sump was cleaned. Then came the second floods. Again, Dr Bala stopped admissions and referred her patients as usual to the nearby Bloom Hospital.

The third time, a warning of heavy rainfall was issued towards the end of November, and Dr Bala did not take in any patients for an entire week. After waiting for a week, when the sun was out and the hospital had been cleaned and there was no sign of rains, she decided to start admitting patients again. There were four patients, all about to deliver in under a day or two. One was to deliver twins, one was pregnant with a child who had growth retardation, and a third was in breech; each patient had a different complication.

It began to drizzle at around 6 in the evening on 1 December. Around 6.30 p.m. there was a heavy downpour. She sent a patient back home, who had come from far away, in the hospital's ambulance. By 7.30 p.m., the rain really picked up. That's when Dr Bala decided to shift everyone out. She called nearby hospitals, and all of them said they couldn't send a vehicle down to her hospital. She called the fire service, the local councillor, the MLA, assistant commissioners of police … everyone she possibly could. Every single person said they couldn't come or said they would try and hung up, to never call back.

'I told them this is a hospital. Patients who are to deliver are inside and if some more time passes I can't even shift them. I pleaded with them to help so I can just move them from this low area to a few hundred metres away. Nobody came.'

By 8 p.m., she was sitting in knee-deep water. She folded her legs up on her chair. 'I could see scorpions and snakes right under my feet.'

'No one came through. I was desperate. A lot of tension was building up inside me. I could just feel it. To add to my problems, the electricity went off.' The hospital did have a generator but that too went under water.

Every year during the rains, she moves all her equipment to a higher floor. That year she couldn't move just one equipment, and it was destroyed in the floods.

There was no power, no backup, there were four patients in labour and there was no way of shifting any of them out. She finally called Bloom and asked them to do something.

'Get somebody. A big van with high wheels. Even if the engine doesn't work, all of us, the hospital staff, will push the vehicle to that place,' she pleaded again, because her patients couldn't walk in the water on the streets. 'I said, I don't care how much it costs. I will pay whatever it takes.'

Finally, Bloom came through and they managed to send someone over. Around 11.30 in the night, four hours after she started looking for help, a van arrived. 'I said to the van driver, "Today, you are God. Safely take these people, patients and their attendants, to the other hospital." And he did. Amazingly.'

But first, even within the hospital, the four patients had to wade through the floodwater. Dr Bala sent them off with their reports and with instructions to remove all their clothes, take a shower and wear new clothes, and reassured them that good doctors would take care of them in Bloom.

Two patients who had already delivered were also in the hospital. She gave them candles, water and food. They had to be in the hospital overnight; the staff and Dr Bala stayed with them. The next morning, they too were sent away in the same van.

'We were caught unaware this time. It was not the rainfall. There was no warning whatsoever. We were warned only of a rain one whole week ago and that too had lapsed.'

'Who warns you usually?' I asked. 'Does some intimation come?'

'No. No. No.' She shook her head. 'The warning comes from my news watching. I see if it will rain and decide for myself if we are going to be flooded. That's how it has always been. We don't get any communication from the government, ever.'

'So no flood warning?'

'Nothing.

'You want to hear something that's worse, something that makes me angry still? Everything had dried up and we had begun operations after this whole fiasco, when they came to do "flood relief" work. They brought along a water bottle that had Amma's face on it and milk powder. I asked, "For whose death have you brought this milk?" Twenty days after a flood, to a hospital, they are giving us one-litre water bottle and one milk powder packet. What sort of government is this? Nobody even came to ask us what happened, even afterwards.'

On the morning after the floods, once the patients had been shifted, Dr Bala and her thirty-five nurses moved to her apartment close by, and they managed by cooking and eating whatever was available. But even after two days, there was no sign of the water receding. Nobody's phone was working. There was no drinking water. Like most of Chennai, they too were using rainwater for everything.

'We used the floodwater that was all over to flush the toilets because we needed the rainwater for washing our faces and brushing.' Soon, the kitchen stocks too diminished. Dr Bala decided to send her then twenty-eight-year-old daughter Ghana, to check on the situation outside and to bring some rations back from the hospital. She left at 2 p.m. and there was no sign of Ghana until 5 p.m.

'It usually takes less than fifteen minutes to complete this trip. I was worried about her.'

Ghana had to swim through the streets to reach the hospital and use a large tub to carry the rations.

Once the waters receded, the hospital had to be scrubbed clean and Dr Bala had the entire place fumigated. Twice. The hospital resumed operations after a fortnight. For an entire month there was no income, but there were additional expenses. 'Forget compensation, there wasn't anyone from the government's side to help us during the emergency. That's what irks me.'

Dr Bala now has a Force Gurkha, famous for its 4x4x4 feature—four wheeler for all four seasons and all four types of terrains. The ambulance they already had was a low vehicle and not suited for extreme weather conditions. She zeroed in on the Gurkha so that at least transporting people out during floods would be in her control. In this area, land prices are unimaginably high today, and yet, one needs vehicles fit for traversing difficult terrain in geographically remote places. The irony is not lost on Dr Bala.

'There is no semblance of planning in this area,' she said. Every inch of land has been sold and buildings have come up choc-a-bloc. Poor stormwater drain maintenance and the dumping of construction rubble from large buildings on canals and drains, obstructing the flow of water, Dr Bala said, are regular occurrences in this neighbourhood, which recently saw the opening of a luxury mall, the Palladium.

'If something had happened to those patients, that would have been the end of my career.' Dr Bala's voice trembled and she blinked off tears. 'Even if it wasn't my responsibility ...' She could no longer stop the tears. 'I have pregnant mothers here.'

'I was fine then, but now that I think about it, I am choking up. It would have been really bad if something had gone wrong. God saved me.'

Sources, Statements and Silence

Speculations were rife in Tamil Nadu, during and after the floods, that not even senior officers from the police or the electricity board were cautioned about the possible scale of devastation that was to unfold on that horrible day. The state does have rules, even if outdated, about the protocol that must be followed when brimming reservoirs are opened and its banks are expected to flood.

In response to an RTI that I had filed with the Public Works Department (PWD)—the ministry in charge of the water bodies, which has been largely held responsible for the floods—asking when its officers were informed about the opening of the city's reservoirs on 1 December, the department said that this information was not 'required to be given' to its staff. Throwing caution to the wind, officials seemed to be signalling that rules were not for them. Their answer is patently false. Rule 2.05 of the 'Compendium of Rules of Regulation on Floods of Tamil Nadu', a document prepared in October 1984, on the protocol to be followed if the Chembarambakkam Reservoir floods, requires information to be sent to a list of officers on the event of flooding. This includes the Chief Engineer of Irrigation, PWD; Superintending Engineer, Chengalpattu circle PWD; Executive Engineer, Saidapet PWD; Sub-Divisional Officer, Saidapet subdivision PWD; Chengalpattu and Madras District Collectors; Madras Commissioner of Police; Madras Commissioner of Corporation; and General Manager, Southern Railway.

According to a report by Arun Janardhanan, who covered the floods extensively for *The Indian Express*,[45] many of the officers who should have been informed were kept in the dark. 'Sources in the police, electricity board and revenue department were, however, livid that they were not made aware of such a huge release. "As on any other rainy day, our teams did the customary evacuation of a few families from the river banks that evening," said a revenue officer. He questioned why the excess water was released at night, catching many asleep and helpless. An angry official, who claimed he would seek voluntary retirement, said, "They all took it lightly. At a meeting convened after the floods, members just blamed the unprecedented rain." A police officer said, "Had they informed us by 7 p.m. at least, we could have sent our men to various localities to alert residents. All stations in the city have at least four or five vehicles."'

In his article, Janardhanan showed just how grave this flood was, how big a lapse in procedure the entire charade was and how 2 December, the morning after the release of water, unfolded. 'Over the rest of the day, there was no sign of government machinery on the ground. Reports came of families of defence and police officials, including security officers of the chief minister, themselves being stranded. Communication remained down.'

I spoke to Janardhanan and asked him about his impressions from his time on the ground. He said, 'The flood happened because of administrative problems. They didn't manage the water levels and had to open the shutters finally. Usually,

Chennai "floods" in an hour and drains in six. Waterlogging is there, but this kind of flooding? No.'

Whatever can possibly go wrong in India, happened in this one event, he said. 'We don't have proper systems. By the time the flooding started, the police force had gone home. They lost communication with each other; no advance measures were made; army and navy were clueless mainly because there was no coordination between the state government and the Centre; [there were] no safety gears, not even adequate number of boats, not many people for rescue operations. This is how the entire mess unfolded. If this kind of calamity happens again, this exact same chaos will play out again. See what happened with Cyclone Ockhi and how it was managed by the southern states? Even in Kerala, Ockhi was not handled well at all and people were very angry.'

The impact of the floods was worse, Janardhanan said, in places like the town of Cuddalore, 175 kilometres to the south of Chennai, where farmers could not even figure out where they had cultivated, because all the debris the flood had left behind was piled up on the fields. They could not determine where a canal began and ended and where their own plots lay.

'There were lapses. They are still there in almost every other thing we do. In the Thoothukudi shooting too [when the police shot to death thirteen protestors and injured several others who were demonstrating against the Sterlite factory on 22 May 2018[46]], for instance, the government had no mechanism for mob control.'

Janardhanan pointed out that the then ruling AIADMK was, as is common knowledge, a centralised party, with zero democracy and with no second-rung leaders. 'We definitely cannot compare ourselves to Scandinavian countries here. The larger issue is that we don't know how to govern.'

A lot has been written in praise of TN's administrative superiority and great bureaucracy in the past, and rightly so too, perhaps. But these floods laid threadbare the problems inherent to the kind of governance followed in TN: the vindictiveness of one government in discontinuing programmes started by the previous one; shunting officers, expecting party-cadre-like loyalty from them; and officers who, indeed, act like they are party cadre.

The chinks in TN's administrative armour became apparent in the manner in which the water was released from the reservoir.

According to an investigation on the floods by the news portal *Firstpost*,[47] 'Since more than 500 mm rainfall was predicted over 1 and 2 December, bringing down the level of water in the [Chembarambakkam] reservoir from 22 to 18 feet—so that it could absorb the downpour—appeared to be a viable solution. Since the Adyar was also comparatively dry because of scanty rainfall before November, the authorities were convinced that the water could be successively diverted with this pre-emptive measure. But the proposal became mired in bureaucratic wrangling and the sluice gates could not be opened before the rain started. "By the time permission was granted by the chief secretary, it was too late," a senior TN government official told *Firstpost*, requesting that his name be withheld as he is not authorised to speak to the media. When it began to rain, the reservoir overflowed within hours. Panicking officials opened the sluice gates, hoping Adyar would absorb the gushing water. But soon its embankments were overrun. The swollen river soon inundated the city.'

A report by Sandhya Ravishankar on 10 December for *The Wire,* too, quoted anonymous sources within the government: 'Although an alarm was sounded off to release water from the brimming Chembarambakkam Reservoir on 30 November itself, the secretary of the Public Works Department awaited a green signal from the chief secretary of the state. The chief secretary, in turn, appears to have delayed the nod. What is mysterious is why the state's top bureaucrat was even involved in what should have been such a routine matter.'

Journalists Dhanya Rajendran and S. Ramanathan of *The News Minute* spoke to an unnamed PWD engineer who was at the Chembarambakkam on the night of the floods. This engineer too, like the PWD principal secretary, N.S. Palaniappan, rejected the claim that bureaucratic delay was the cause for the floods, and instead said that it was 'nature's fury' that had caused it. According to *The News Minute* report, 'On that night, at least one chief engineer, one senior engineer and one assistant engineer were present at the lake apart from the regular staff. The senior officials had gone to the lake to monitor the situation between midnight on 1 December and 5 a.m. on 2 December.... On 1 December, as the day progressed, the inflow of water into the lake increased due to the rains, and correspondingly the outflow of water from the lake to the Adyar river was increased.... According to the engineer, 6 p.m. was the major breaking point when the water level reached dangerous levels. The engineer says that water was never released beyond 29,000 cusecs.'

The engineer sounds hurt and defensive: 'It is wrong to say that we should have released the water earlier, even if we had emptied the entire Chembarambakkam Lake and kept it, the water would have filled up in just a day. The inflow was very high. ... We saved the reservoir, and we restricted the outflow to 29,000 cusecs so that too much water does not flow into the river. We were getting about 31,000 cusecs of inflow till 6 in the morning, but we never crossed the limit.'[48]

That the late chief minister, J. Jayalalithaa, ran a tight ship and did not allow anyone to speak to the press was indeed well known. It was also common for newspapers to be slapped with criminal defamation cases. (Things have gone from bad to worse in TN since her demise, with journalists being arrested and dissenters and protestors being shot to death.) It was obvious that in spite of this, authorities and officials from various departments were exchanging blames and barbs hiding behind anonymous quotes in various news outlets through the course of the floods.

Unmindful of the defamation suits that were sure to come their way, several news organisations did their best to find out what had gone wrong during the floods and notably, many of these media houses were victims of the floods themselves. *The Hindu,* for instance, was not published for the first time in its history as its staff could not reach the printing press in Maraimalar Nagar, and several news channels had to stop telecast as they were flooded.[49]

Ravishankar's piece for *The Wire* also quoted sources within the Chennai Corporation and the police to show that information reached them only around 8 p.m. on 1 December, just four hours before the banks flooded and after the release of 29,000 cusecs of water. Neither the coast guard nor the Tamil Nadu Generation and Distribution Corporation Limited (TANGEDCO), which supplies electricity to the city, were informed. A senior police officer, quoted in Ravishankar's report, said that even a central control room was not set up by the TN police and that 'each agency was doing its own thing'.

The army, navy, air force and coast guard coordinated with each other informally. A coast guard officer, quoted in Ravishankar's article, again anonymously, said: 'We got calls from the public and we moved to those areas based on calls received. At the ground level, our personnel coordinated with police personnel on the ground.'

The consensus among all the government officials in-charge in the aftermath of the floods seemed to be that waiting for a nod from 'up above' had caused the floods.

The then chief secretary of the state, K. Gnanadesikan, however, rubbished it all in a press release on 13 December. 'As heavy rain was forecast, supervisory officers including the chief engineer, Chennai Region of Water Resources Organisation, Public Works Department were also present at Chembarambakkam tank and personally monitoring the situation. The engineers in charge of the tank closely monitored the inflows and the rainfall in the upstream catchment area and accordingly regulated the discharge from the tank for the purpose of ensuring the safety of the tank.' He further claimed that no specific instructions or orders were sought from senior officers or the PWD about the release from the Chembarambakkam in the period leading up to 1 December.

Even as report after report in the press sought to lay the blame for the delay in the opening of the Chembarambakkam's sluice gates at the chief secretary's office, was it appropriate of him to have released this statement, giving himself as well as others a clean chit, instead of subjecting all involved, including himself, to at least an official enquiry? The tone of his press statement sounded like a threat, replete with words like 'malicious' and 'canards', as if it would soon be followed by defamation suits. Perhaps it was drafted by a legal team, aimed at sounding righteous as well as like a veiled threat.

Explaining the 'logical' steps that were responsible for this flooding, the chief secretary said: 'Based on the field situation, the engineers on the spot increased the outflow to 10,000 cusecs at 10 a.m., 12,000 cusecs at 12 noon and to 20,960 cusecs from 2 p.m. in the afternoon. This outflow was further increased to 25,000 cusecs at 5 p.m. and to 29,000 cusecs at 6 p.m. based on the inflows and maintained at that level till 3 p.m. next day and reduced gradually. It is thus abundantly clear that the engineers present at the Chembarambakkam tank site had taken the required decision based on the inflow into the reservoir. Similarly, water was being released from many other tanks and reservoirs including Red Hills, Cholavaram and Poondi as a result of heavy inflow for which the local controlling officers took the decisions. Hence, the allegation that they were waiting for instructions from the Principal Secretary, Public Works Department and the Chief Secretary and the imputation that the officers were awaiting the clearance from the Hon'ble Chief Minister are malicious and are canards not supported by the water release data of the reservoir.'

There were several discrepancies within this clarification that he had issued. For instance, in one part of his long statement, he said, 'The engineers on the spot increased the outflow to 10,000 cusecs at 10 a.m., 12,000 cusecs at 12 noon and to 20,960 cusecs from 2 p.m. in the afternoon.' And in another part of the same press release, he said, 'The Collector of Chennai issued a first flood warning when the discharge reached 7,500 cusecs at 11.20 a.m. on 1.12.2015.'

Which was it? 7500 cusecs at 11.20 a.m. or 10,000 cusecs as early as 10 a.m.? According to a certified copy of the log extract of the Chembarambakkam Reservoir that I accessed, the outflow at 10 a.m. on 1 December 2018 was 10,000 cusecs.

Just as there was a paucity of official information on the floods, it seems that there was confusion on just how much water was released from the Chembarambakkam and how much water was flowing through the Adyar.

~

Some sources indicated to me that the floods happened at a time that was 'the beginning of the end' in a sense, as far as Jayalalithaa was concerned, and that senior officers in the police force and secretaries of the state themselves had little direct access to her.

The then PWD minister, O. Panneerselvam, was infamous for being Amma's 'loyal' lieutenant. He began almost all his sentences with paeans to his leader: '*Maanbumigu mudhal amaichar, puratchi thalaivi Amma avargalin aanaikinanga*,' meaning, 'On the orders of the honourable chief minister, revolutionary leader Amma.' That his ministry depended on Poes Garden—Jayalalithaa's 'official home' from where she often conducted her duties—before 'okaying' even a small decision, is common knowledge in the power corridors of TN.

If the flood was caused because PWD officials were waiting for permission from Poes Garden, whose permission were our elected officials and executives waiting for if Jayalalithaa was unwell? She was out of action by December 2015, my sources speculated, and there were rumours that she was not running the government. The government was more or less run by V.K. Sasikala, who was a close aide of Jayalalithaa, and officers also largely preferred to brief her, they said. Many newspapers were sent criminal defamation notices for just speculating about Jayalalithaa's health throughout 2015 (over 200 such cases were filed by the AIADMK between 2011 and 2016). A member of parliament from the party had even said that he would cut off the tongues of anyone who dared to speak about Jayalalithaa's health.

That Sasikala had control over the state as the 'unofficial deputy CM', the Chinnamma (little mother) to Jayalalithaa's Amma, was reported in the news, way back in December 2011, when there was a public spat between Jayalalithaa and Sasikala. But the duo eventually patched up. Deposing before an inquiry commission on Jayalalithaa's death, J. Krishnapriya, Sasikala's niece, said in January 2018 that Sasikala was so influential before the 2011 spat that she handpicked not only candidates for elections but even officers, including collectors, police officers and secretaries. Even their transfers were carried out under her instructions. (Krishnapriya's mother is currently serving a jail term, along with Sasikala, after being convicted in the disproportionate assets case by the Supreme Court in 2017.) Krishnapriya also said that post-2011, Sasikala's influence had 'reduced considerably'.

However, there is reason to believe that Sasikala continued to hold more power than other elected officials and bureaucrats of the state,[50] even as Jayalalithaa's health took a turn for the worse. An example of Sasikala's influence was demonstrated early in 2018, when the Income Tax Department told the Madras High Court that a secret letter it had written to the then director general of police (DGP), Ashok Kumar, and chief secretary, P. Rama Mohan Rao, in August 2016, about bribes paid to the health minister in the 'Gutka scam' in TN, was found in Sasikala's room in Poes Garden, when the room was raided in November 2017. It was accompanied by a note from the then DGP, addressed to the chief minister of TN.[51]

In July 2015, Jayalalithaa released a short statement, citing health reasons for not being able to attend former President Abdul Kalam's funeral: 'I have great affection and respect for Abdul Kalam. I would like to attend his funeral and pay my respects to him. However, owing to my health condition I am not in a position to travel.' Her absence in the secretariat as well as in public events, such as the signing of MoUs and iftar parties, had also been noticed by the people and the press.[52] Some said it was her diabetes, while others said it was her kidneys and yet others, her thyroid.

Delhi-based journalist Arvind Gunasekar, while commenting on the political scenario in TN back in 2015, which was dramatically different from what it is like today, said, 'Tamil Nadu is the only state in this country where the opening of a reservoir is a political act. Everywhere else a junior engineer would be tasked with it. But here, the chief minister releases press statements about it. Ministers go to shower flowers when they are opened etc.'

Those of us in TN know this to be a fact. The opening of reservoirs and the act of providing water for drinking or irrigation have been spun by politicians as acts of individual graces and bravado. As if leaders have to go out of their way to fight and bring us water. This also has to be seen in the backdrop of the water disputes TN is embroiled in—the Cauvery water dispute with Karnataka as well as the Mullaperiyar Dam issue with the other neighbouring state Kerala. Elections are won and fought over who brought water.

The AIADMK government, during the floods, had the peculiar problem of too many cooks in the kitchen. Not one of them, however, took responsibility for the disaster they had created. Jayalalithaa, apart from being 'guided' by Sasikala, was also guided by three former bureaucrats, and those serving as secretaries in various departments. There is no way to clearly point to any one person and say, 'Their actions caused the floods'. 'In fact, it was inaction that caused the floods,' Gunasekar argued.

Perhaps, swayed by the fact that water is such an emotional issue to the people of Chennai and, perhaps, in a bid to save water for the summer months—when large parts of the city experience acute shortage and most homes survive on water that comes in for only a few hours during the day—those in charge during the floods waited too long before letting precious resources out of the reservoir until very late. And then in a state of panic, they let it all out in one go, inundating the city.

This is exactly why an emergency action plan for a reservoir is important. It takes the moral quandary out of the equation and allows engineers on the ground to take a call, keeping safety as well as future requirements in mind. If there was a plan, there would have been no need for this sort of panic. There still seems to be no such plan, almost four years after the floods. Even after the entire capital city of one of India's biggest states drowned.

~

In this backdrop of sycophancy, fear and absolute lack of transparency, it was not only the reasons for the floods that were glossed over but also information about the loss incurred during the floods. (A year after the floods, when Jayalalithaa passed away on 5 December 2016, her own death was mired in confusion, chaos and lack of information. Later, a controversy erupted with factions within her party levelling charges against each other over her death. Enquiry commissions were formed and court cases filed. In fact, it was Panneerselvam who first raised doubts over Jayalalithaa's death, after his public revolt against Sasikala.)

The TN government waited over a month after the floods until 4 January, to release the final numbers of the lives lost. Even then, the state only gave the numbers of those dead during the northeast monsoon period, between the months of October and December across the state, rather than specific data on those who had died in the December deluge. The statement from the chief minister said that during the northeast monsoon period, between 1 and 27 October, 49 persons died and between 28 October and 31 December, 421 persons died due to various reasons, including drowning, electrocution, lightning strike and wall collapse.

On 7 December 2015, the TN government announced its flood compensation package, which included 10,000 houses—which meant more people would be moved out of the city's river banks into vertical slums built on wetlands and flood-prone places far away from the city in areas like Okkiyam, Thoraipakkam and Perumbakkam—and monetary assistance between ₹5,000 and ₹10,000 per household to be made as a direct cash transfer to banks. The package also included 10 kilos of rice and one dhoti and one saree that was distributed through the city's Public Distribution System. While the chief minister said that 245 families of persons who had died in the floods had been given ₹4 lakh each as compensation, there is no further mention of any other form of compensation given to the victims apart from the ₹5000 and ₹10,000 assistance.

Compare this to the losses across the state:

According to the government's statement, over 1 lakh livestock perished as did crops over an area of 3.83 lakh hectares, affecting the livelihoods of 68,350 farmers, during the monsoon of 2015.

Other official reports have indicated that paddy, millets, pulses, cotton, sugarcane, oilseeds and horticultural crops and plantations were destroyed and agricultural lands were further damaged by sand casting and heavy siltation. 112 primary health care centres, 124 higher secondary schools, 11 medical colleges, 334 noon-meal centres, 320 mechanised boats, 571 FRP vallams (fibre-reinforced plastic canoes), 445 catamarans, 5274 fishing nets were damaged by the floods. 3964 handloom weavers were affected as their looms, accessories and materials were damaged, while 726 potters lost potters' wheels and other implements of pottery as well as finished goods across Cuddalore, Kanchipuram, Thiruvannamalai, Erode and Villupuram. Nearly 27 lakh homes were submerged across Chennai, Cuddalore, Thiruvallur and Kancheepuram. And one cannot put a value to a lifetime's worth of savings of hundreds of low- and middle-income families that were washed away in the floods.[53]

The floods also crippled the state's micro, small and medium enterprises (MSMEs).

Among industries, they are the most vulnerable and generate a high number of jobs, many of which go to those in the marginalised communities. In effect, when our MSMEs are sick, they hit the poor the most. Various estimates point out that at least 2 lakh workers were affected and that the sector might have needed a minimum of ₹10,000 crore to get back to where it was before the floods. Over 2,000 MSMEs were affected by the floods. Many MSMEs have no access to formal lenders and are forced to go to private institutions for capital.

Chennai-based business journalist Jude Sannith told me, 'Tamil Nadu's MSMEs have had the short end of the stick in the last couple of years. The Federation of Indian Chambers of Commerce and Industry [FICCI] went on record with an estimated loss figure of ₹3,000 to 4,000 crore, which it based solely on estimates from industrial estates in Ambattur and Guindy in Chennai, and Kancheepuram, Thiruvallur and Vellore districts.' FICCI's presidential advisor, P. Murari, told Sannith, 'But this is only a rough estimate. It could be even more.' The estimates also suggested that MSMEs across TN and Puducherry had also suffered devastating losses. Small pharma plants were running losses in the range of ₹200 crore, with the lurking possibility of that number going all the way up to ₹1,200 crore.

Sources in the Small and Tiny Industries Association also pegged their losses in TN and Puducherry at ₹1,000 crore. 'The Ambattur Industrial Estate had also written to Indian Overseas Bank, requesting a six-month breather to repay a medium-term loan,' Sannith said. 'The tragedy of the flood, though, was that it was merely a precursor of things to come. The next year saw Tamil Nadu encounter a tumultuous three months, politically, when Jayalalithaa took ill, to pass away in December. Reports of policy paralysis during this period spread thick and fast. Cyclone Vardah arrived a few days after the chief minister's demise [in 2016], to cause another minor hiccup just when things began looking up. Not long after, a sustained period of political uncertainty, instability and lack of legislative leadership in the state government further dented the recovery prospects of the sector.'

~

As late as April 2018, over two years after the flood, police claimed to have found the body of a young man who had been washed away by the floods on 1 December. Arun Kumar and Azaruddin, both AC mechanics and residents of Anjugam Nagar, waded through neck-deep water to leave their homes that night. Azaruddin's body was found completely decomposed, forty days later. Police claimed in April 2018 that they thought that a skeleton and skull lying in the bushes around the Adyar Canal, found by the locals, was in fact that of Arun Kumar's. They would further claim that, incredulously, all this time later, an ID card of Arun Kumar's had been found near the skeleton.[54]

Newspaper reports from the time of the floods peg the number of deaths, quoting police sources, just during that week in December as 514, with maximum casualties from Chennai and two neighbouring districts.[55] The Royapettah Government Hospital alone saw fifty dead bodies being brought in from various parts of the city, between 1 and 7 December, most of whom had died from drowning, according to a report in *The News Minute* by Pheba Mathew. On 3 December, even in the midst of the flooding, when the water hadn't begun to recede, Rajnath Singh, the home minister of the country, had said that 269 people died in the rains.[56] There was, however, no clarity on the final number as news reports from the time also said that real figures were only forthcoming off the record.

I decided to wade in to find out, for this book, how many hundreds it was in reality. It felt like the most basic fact, one that must be definitely readily available. Right? Wrong.

I filed a query under the RTI Act to find out the exact number of casualties due to the Chennai floods between 1 and 5 December 2015. The reply from the tahsildar, Disaster Management, Chennai Collectorate was: 'w.r.t the information about no. of persons died in the flooding between 01.12.2015 to 05.12.2015, it is informed that 38 persons died due to 2015 flood in Chennai District...'.

Thirty-eight is the official number that the Chennai administration is maintaining. Not 512 as the newspapers had reported. Not 269 as the home minister had claimed.

I asked journalist Mathew, who had worked extensively on the ground during the floods and interviewed several people, some who had lost relatives to the waters, about this number.

'This is way low,' she said, 'Absolutely not possible. Sources within Royapettah and Kilpauk hospitals alone told me that they saw fifty bodies each that week. If the number were a bit closer to what I saw on the ground I would still believe it but this doesn't even come close.'

If RTI does not yield the right number even of the dead, from a catastrophe like this, where should one look? Between the sources who fear for their promotions, safety and very life and the highly unreliable answers that come forth on record—somewhere in this strange spectrum lies the truth. About who we lost and how we lost them in December 2015.

I, unfortunately, failed in my endeavour to find out just which of these numbers was real.

Death of Dignity

People of this city took everything the floods threw their way in their stride. The one thing they couldn't deal with was just how the river and all those responsible for its rage had robbed not only lives but also the dignity of those who had lost their lives. The trauma of not being able to lay a loved one to rest, in peace, is not one that can be easily forgotten, or forgiven. And none were spared this ignominy in death, not the poor, not the rich, not the super-rich.

Tragedy, unlike lightning, it seems, can strike the people of Chennai repeatedly. R. Gokul Krishnan, who works as a stonecutter, and his twin siblings R. Keerthana and R. Keertha who work in a grocery store, are testament to this. Relocated out of their homes under duress following the tsunami of 2004, they came to Semmenchery with their mother Nalini, having lost their father earlier to a heart attack. On 1 December, Nalini was heading back from Manapakkam's MIOT Hospital where she worked, to ensure her home wasn't flooded and that her children were safe. She was lost to the raging river forever.

Nalini's children didn't know just what had happened for five agonising days even as they looked in hospitals and police stations for her. She was floating in a lake, where fishermen found her and informed the police. This is something that recurred far too many times during the flood. Fishermen rescuing people, fishermen fishing out bodies, fishermen informing the police about the bodies ... The fishermen of Chennai doing the work the state was supposed to.

Nalini's children, along with a social worker, had to engage in a long tussle with the bureaucracy to lay claim to her body, just as Lt Col G. Venkatesan's family had had to. Venkatesan was laid on the roadside and later a wrong body was handed over to his daughter and son-in-law, before the right one was, and they had to travel all the way to Triplicane, eleven kilometres away, to cremate him. Just as Nalini's corpse was seen by her children, bloated and covered in worms, in the mortuary, alongside those of others fished out of lakes and rivers, before she was cleaned and taken to a crematorium. The ordeal ended only when Nalini's children coughed up ₹4,000 as a bribe to see their mother off with dignity.[57]

In the wee hours of 4 September, six coaches of the Chennai–Mangalore Express had derailed as it approached the Poovanur station. Most of those injured were treated as outpatients at the Vridachalam Government Hospital.[58] Fifty-three-year-old Paranjyothi suffered from injuries to her right shoulder and a serious internal wound and was being treated at MIOT. By December, she was incapable of breathing properly as her lungs had steadily filled up with fluid, and she was on ventilator support.

Her son, unable to reach the hospital because of the floods and with phone lines cut off, tried to reach her through various sources. He had heard a rumour that ICU patients of the hospital were transferred to the nearby Ramachandra Hospital. He was not able to get there, either.

On 4 December, however, he learnt from private news channels that fourteen people had died at MIOT and that their bodies were being brought to the Royapettah Government Hospital. He visited the Royapettah Hospital just to make sure his mother was not among them. Unfortunately for him, her name figured in that list.[59]

At MIOT, eighteen patients died in the critical care unit between 2 and 3 December. Among the eighteen, was one-year-old Jude Immanuel Bijoy. He died before reaching Ramachandra, after being shifted out of MIOT's cardiothoracic ICU. Doctors at the hospital manually pumped oxygen for critically ill patients and tried to manage without power supply, which meant there was no way to monitor their vitals.[60]

Senior advocate and human rights activist Sudha Ramalingam was admitted to MIOT and spent the fateful night of the floods along with two members of her family in darkness, save for some candles. She saw the staff in the hospital do their best even as the administration's apathy distressed her and other patients. Following a critical surgery, she spent the day and night of the floods in the hospital. All this without power backup, under extremely unsterile conditions, bitten by mosquitoes all night, listening to the cries and moans of others from different corners of the hospital, even as her friends, family and colleagues, who could not be with her in the hospital, were in panic, not knowing how she was or if she was even around anymore. 'There wasn't even water to drink. And not only were the other patients in my ward old, even their caretakers were senior citizens. My caretakers took on the role of helping everyone there,' she told me later. She recalled that the hospital management sent crates of mineral water bottles to the block where international patients were admitted and didn't send any to the Indian patients. Her caretakers fought with the administration and finally secured some water for the patients and distributed it. Eventually, Ramalingam's doctor arranged for an ambulance to transfer her to another hospital, and she was injured during the bumpy transit. After close to three years, even though her surgical scars have disappeared, the scar from the wound caused during that transit hasn't. She showed it to me when I went to speak to her about the floods.

By the evening of 3 December, the MIOT administration decided to move patients, through the floods. Under heat from relatives of the dead, and the national media that had, after ignoring the flooding in Chennai, finally started reporting on these deaths, the state's health secretary and MIOT's management exchanged barbs and tried to blame each other. The government said that the hospital failed in its job to have enough backup (their backup generators were flooded) and that led to deaths. The hospital said that they had no warning, that no one had come to rescue the hundreds stuck inside and that those who had died had collapsed due to their illness over the two days of the flood and not because of the power backup failure.[61]

In the other end of town, in Nandanam, sixty-three-year-old Dr Girijashankar, on vacation from Florida, left his home to buy medicine for his ailing ninety-year-old mother. His wife and family looked everywhere for him for two days, including in hospitals. Forty-eight hours later, as the waters receded, they found his body wrapped around a scooter in his mother's building. Though the water levels had been low near his home just two streets away, it had hurtled like a raging storm and brought a compound wall down close to where he was found dead.

As the city flooded, so did its cemeteries and crematoriums. Over at the historic Quibble Island Cemetery, near MRC Nagar, water was so high that none of the tombs—neither the centuries-old ones nor the new ones—or the crosses could be seen. Everything had been damaged, and caretaker Paulraj spent weeks clearing out the rotten grass and damaged plants all around. In the aftermath of the 2015 deluge, several families had to repair the graves of loved ones. Paulraj and his family had taken refuge in the nearby Santhome Church during the floods.

MRC Nagar, located behind the cemetery, is mere metres away from the Adyar Estuary. In the past, conservationists had warned many times that the high-rise buildings and unchecked construction of both government and private-owned structures in this sensitive region would not bode well. However, these alarm bells went unheeded. The river's flow into the sea, near MRC Nagar, was blocked by these buildings, and this led to the drowning of Quibble Island and its historic landmark. The floods didn't spare even the long dead.

Writing for *Scroll.in* on the December music season and the Chennai floods that had disrupted it and sent many an artiste into a moral dilemma on whether to perform during that December or not, pianist Anil Srinivasan said he had no such dilemmas. 'On a fateful evening just a week ago, I had to stand guard for about nineteen corpses that surfaced after two feet of water drained away. Ragas? I asked. You've got to be kidding me ...'[62] Srinivasan also said that any amount of virtuosic playing was not going to help him 'face the horror of trying to find folks to claim bodies left behind.'

In Ashok Nagar, a young woman sat alone in her house through the night with her dead mother's body, plunged into darkness following a long power shutdown, as the city flooded around her. She was unable to move, unable to cremate, unable to even bring in blocks of ice or freezer boxes to preserve the body.[63]

Gravediggers had to work extra hard in the days following the floods, even as they dealt with badly decayed bodies that floated to the surface after burial, as rainwater had soaked up the graves. Over a hundred corpses were sent for burial in the week following the floods to a ground whose average body count per week until then was five. As late as 7 December, cremation grounds in and around the city were flooded, further choking up those that were functional.[64]

Industrialist M.A.M. Ramaswamy, the last 'Rajah of Chettinad' and chairman of the Chettinad Group of Companies, and whose Chettinad Palace abuts the Adyar River, died due to an illness on the evening of 2 December, at a hospital in Adyar. He could be cremated only four days later, the following Sunday, when power returned to the Besant Nagar crematorium.[65]

The city's grievance, repeated over and over again to me by its various inhabitants, was not with the flood, at all. In the sense that, we all accept floods as a part of natural phenomenon that wreaks havoc. Our problem was with the manner in which it was handled by the state. That the state cut off power supply, did not give most of the city any warning, opened up reservoirs and let out an extraordinary amount of water, even as its people was thrown into a void, where there was neither information nor light. Just darkness. And then in the dead of the night, the killer waters just came in and took whatever they wanted. Whatever they could lay their hands on. Lives of people, solitary breadwinners, pets, animals, trees and families. Sending people back in their status by at least a decade or two, killing all of their precious memories, the things they spent a large part of their adulthood buying and saving, on EMIs or chit funds, in some cases, families' entire belongings, the almirahs of the poor that had anything worth anything, all of their cash, saved up in one place or various places in the house, in the kitchen, in some hundi, some money meant as offering to gods, small and medium businesses in industrial estates that submerged entirely and with it the hopes and dreams of many a first-generation entrepreneur ...

It's legacy included widows, widowers, orphans, parents who had lost their only child, heartbroken and tragically separated lovers, jobless people, homeless poor, the displaced, the marginalised, barren fields, closed factories, losses to manufacturers that would continue to have a ripple effect and cost the Indian economy 3 billion dollars.

Memories of Kosasthalaiyar

Attirambakkam village is an 'open-air Palaeolithic site situated near a meandering tributary stream of the river Kortallaiyar, [known variously as Cortelliar or Kosasthalaiyar], north-west of Chennai, Tamil Nadu, along the south-east coast of India. Discovered in September 1863, by Robert Bruce Foote and his colleague William King, it was investigated in the early to mid-20th century by several scholars.'[66] Attirambakkam is just sixty-one kilometres from Chennai, where 385,000-year-old stone tools have been found. A report in *The Wire* on this astonishing finding said, 'The artefacts recovered from South India are older than the oldest known *Homo sapiens* fossils found in Africa (300,000 years ago). Even the oldest fossils outside Africa—recently reported from Israel—are far younger than those found at Attirampakkam.'[67] Such is the historic significance of the Kosasthalaiyar, whose banks have played an important role in humankind's story. The river originates in Thiruvallur and reaches the Bay of Bengal through the Ennore Creek's backwaters.

In Pattarai Perumbudur village, located on the eastern banks of the Kosasthalaiayar, fifty-seven kilometres from Chennai, among the 200 things discovered so far, dating back to between 2 BCE and 3 CE, two pieces were of significance—a broken piece of rouletted ware, which was a Roman household item, and a perforated conical jar—which proves that TN and Pattarai Perumbudur used to be part of a trade route that connected Romans with the rest of India. News reports from 2018 point out how 'those engaged in excavation were stunned to find the remains of a ring well made of terracotta in the region. They could dig up to the 23rd ring during 2016 excavations, but could not proceed further as water gushed out taking them by surprise.'[68]

The Kosasthalaiyar also played an interesting role in a battle between Hyder Ali and the East India Company's Colonel Baillie. When Baillie reached the northern bank of the Kosasthalaiyar in Pullalur village, on 25 August 1780, the river was dry. Rains that night however caused floods and the Company's forces were detained there for ten days. By the time Baillie's men crossed the river, Ali's son Tipu Sultan was waiting to hand 'by much the greatest disaster that had ever befallen the British arms in India.'[69] The flooding in the river had given Tipu Sultan enough time to prepare for an attack and 'assemble 6,000 horses, 5,000 foot, six heavy guns and a large contingent of Irregulars.'[70]

Over a century later, floods became the norm around the Kosasthalaiyar, as part of the costs colonies paid to the Raj for the railways. The *Macmillan's Magazine* observed in 1878, 'To understand what happens in Southern India during a year of heavy rain reference may be made to the reports of the year 1872.' The magazine quoted the 'Collector of Chingleput' as saying, 'Considerable damage was done to the irrigation works by the heavy floods. ... Keshavaram anicut, at the divergence of Cortelliar and the Cooum ... was almost destroyed by the autumn floods.' How the Kosasthalaiyar came to flood was also explained:[71]

> The Cortelliar is the river principally used for irrigation in this district, and its sources lie in the hills some forty miles from the Coromondel Coast, just where the Eastern Ghats turn west to form the northern boundary of the Carnatic. Twenty-five years ago the slopes and bases of these hills were covered with thick jungles, all of which have been subsequently cut down for use as fuel on the Madras Railway. The consequence of these extensive clearings has been that at the present time the river is in violent flood for as many days during the north-east monsoon as formerly it was in moderate flood during weeks!

Today, the Kosasthalaiyar is one of the sources that feed the Poondi Reservoir, which has a capacity of 3TMC (one thousand million cubic feet). Of the three rivers that traverse Chennai, the Kosasthalaiyar is the largest and the cleanest. It also reaches the sea in a manner most interesting. It does not just flow in but does so only through the Ennore Creek's backwaters, spread over 8,000 acres between the Kattupalli–Ennore Island and the mainland of Chennai. The famous Buckingham Canal that crisscrosses all three rivers of the city also cuts through these backwaters, which are connected to the Pulicat lagoon system. The backwaters, the Ennore Creek and the Pulicat are of great ecological importance and serve as a 'flood sink' by absorbing floodwater during monsoons and gradually discharging them into the sea.

The Coastal Resource Centre (CRC), which provides support to coastal communities, has been at the forefront of protecting what is left of the rights of the fishing communities, who have for long relied on the Ennore Creek for their livelihoods. The Chennai-based organisation is also fighting for the creek itself. The CRC has made it its mission to spread word of the story of Ennore, its past, present as well as future. And this is that story:[72]

> As an arm of the Kosathalaiyar River, the Creek meets the Bay of Bengal at Mugathwara Kuppam, while the northern channel of the creek connects to the Pulicat Lake, the second largest brackish water lake in the country. Six revenue villages namely, Kathivakkam, Ennore, Puzhudhivakkam, Athipattu, Katupalli and Kalanji are located around the Creek. The Ennore Creek, along with the Buckingham Canal and the rest of the Pulicat water system has vast importance for the local fisher folk. The Ennore Creek nurtures a healthy aquatic ecosystem which was once famous for its rich biodiversity. This ecologically sensitive ecosystem was home to large swamps of mangroves that not only ensured a sustainable regeneration of fish resources, but also help mitigate flooding in times of strong rainfall, high tides and cyclones. For decades, this creek sustained the livelihoods of the residents in the surrounding villages and has been demarcated as CRZ (Coastal Regulatory Zone) IV (Water Body) in the coastal zone management plan by the Tamil Nadu State Coastal Zone Management Authority. Undertaking any reclamation, bunding, construction or altering the natural courses of such water bodies is illegal under the CRZ Notification 2011, Water (Prevention and Control of Pollution) Act 1974 and the Environment Protection Act, 1986.

The organisation argues that the 'Ennore Creek can protect us against floods, storms and cyclones and seawater's intrusion into groundwater. That is why it deserves to be declared and protected as a Climate Sanctuary.'[73]

Things were starkly different at Ennore just over a century ago. In fact, back in 1881, Ennore was a famous place of resort. It could be reached 'by a boat plying over the Buckingham's Canal, or by ordinary carriage road through Tondiarpet and Trivettore [Thiruvottriyur]. ... Its chief attraction is a large salt-water lake in which visitors bathe, fish and sail. It has been the scene of many regattas. ... The extensive casuarina plantations that have of late years grown up around the place have much altered its aspect. The lake contains excellent fish and oysters, and salt of a very superior quality is gathered from numerous pans, situated close to the creeks or inlets from the sea. The crystals are large and clear and the quantity gathered annually is about 86 to 40,000 tons. It is the best produced in the Presidency and is shipped in large quantities to Calcutta and other ports.'[74]

Until the turn of the twentieth century, Ennore was a place of great bounty. Scylla serrata or mud crabs were found in large numbers in Madras's markets. Grapsoid crabs and Varuna litterata crabs too abounded in the canals and creeks of the villages here.

The fisherfolk of Ennore are on the verge of losing everything they hold precious, including the biodiversity that once brought them riches. Their loss is Chennai's loss too.

They invited the rest of Chennai through an open letter to save this creek on 2 September 2016:[75]

> We are writing as Chennaiites to Chennaiites to invite you to join us in saving the Ennore Creek. Even as you read this, uncaring people in the government and private sector are harming the river. As fisherfolk, we are the first in the line of fire; the degradation of the creek affects us daily. But this is no

longer merely about us. The river holds the key to our shared environmental fate as a city.

It concerns the flood safety of the very densely populated North Chennai. Those living south of the Cooum may not know that there is a north to Chennai. But we exist—Basin Bridge, Korukkupet, Washermanpet, Thiruvotriyur, Kasimedu, Tondiarpet, Kodungaiyur, Ernavur, Manali, Sadayankuppam, Burma Colony.

Last December, during the floods, even as our villages were under water, our youth were out on boats rescuing people from Ernavur, Manali, Sadayankuppam, Sathyamoorthy Nagar and surrounding areas. We went out in 120 boats and rescued 30,000 people. We know the river, and we know that the reason these areas were flooded is because the river's exit to the sea was blocked by industrial encroachments and pollution.

If you knew the river as well as we do, you will be terrified to hear of what is happening to it, and what the consequences will be for all of us if we allow the damage to continue unchecked.

Neglect in North Chennai

The Buckingham Canal—polluted by the industries situated choc-a-block in the Manali area in North Chennai, raw sewage, ash from a nearby coal power plant, encroachments that have been allowed by the government such as the Kamaraj Port and the construction of pillars and other foundations for the Mass Rapid Transit System (MRTS) trains—has hit the tipping point. Many say it could never be restored.

In its heyday, the canal used to carry goods from the village of Kuruvimedu—kuruvi means sparrow and medu means ridge—which now bears the brunt of poisonous ash from a coal power plant. The ash here and in the neighbouring villages has become one with the water in the pond nearby, and with people's homes and the air they breathe, calling the deep fissures in their lungs its home. The death of Kuruvimedu's network of kalvais or canals, through the Ennore Creek, and with it a way of life—fish, crabs, prawns (vellai iral, karuppu iral, mann iral, irun kezhuthi, madavai, oodan, kezhangan, uppathi, keechan, kalvaan, panna, koduva) catamarans filled with casuarina, salt from Athipattu salt pans,[76] even the kuruvi that once abounded all over Madras—is apparent to anyone who cares to enter the village. In their wake lie ash, coal and oil. Remnants of death.

What I saw in Ennore one overcast morning, accompanied by Pooja Kumar of Coastal Resource Centre, as part of what the organisation calls a 'toxic tour', was appalling. It was as if apocalypse was upon a place less than an hour's drive from the popular Marina Beach. Kumar spoke of the terrifying things happening to the flood sink ecosystem.

The CRC, some time ago, filed RTI queries to request the state government for copies of the Coastal Zone Management Plan's (CZMP) maps based on which the Coastal Zone Regulation (CRZ) clearances were given—which led to huge constructions coming up in this ecologically sensitive area. 'As no new maps were being finalised under the existing CRZ 2011, the government was banking on maps made in 1996 for approvals. We were particularly interested in Ennore as many constructions were already permitted in wetlands. This led to the department of environment disclosing a map that was not in line with the original approved CZMP. There was also no paper trail to show that this map was modified after initial approval. So the fake "modified map" was being used to grant clearances. But this map did not contain the Ennore Creek at all,' Kumar said.

In the Tamil film *Citizen*, an entire village called Athipatti is removed from the Indian map by those in power. TN administrators turned fiction into fact by creating a fake map, removing an entire ecosystem and allowing projects to come up on protected lands.

What needs to be done now? 'The fake map needs to be taken down,' Kumar said. 'All violations of the law should be appraised using the original approved map. And action must be taken on the officers who have been complicit in faking maps and allowing dangerous development.' Even though a case has been filed in the National Green Tribunal (NGT), South Zone, no progress has been made as the NGT is inactive due to non-appointment of judges. What is surprising though, is how little the mainstream national media has investigated a scam of such a large proportion.

The North Chennai Thermal Power Station (NCTPS), in the Katupalli–Ennore Island, dumps toxic fly ash—a remnant of the power production process—into the Kosasthalaiyar River's floodplains, the Buckingham Canal and over 1,000 acres of the backwaters, affecting the entire flood sink and risking North Chennai's ability to help the entire city withstand flooding. A river on whose banks evidence of mankind's most ancient tools have been found, on whose banks civilisation has thrived for hundreds of thousands of years, is now being laid to waste.

The toxic ash from this power plant is transported using pipes to an 'ash pond', where it is stored, before being moved to another facility. The rusted, old pipes that carry this slurry ash leak profusely, dumping large swathes of the ash into the water bodies below. Tidal action washes this ash away from the floodplains into the river, dumping harmful pollutants including nickel, cadmium, antimony, arsenic, chromium, lead and mercury.

Borewell samples taken from Seppakkam, the village west of the ash pond, were severely contaminated with copper, manganese and selenium, apart from the chemicals mentioned above. One of the samples was additionally contaminated with higher levels of molybdenum.

Jayanthi of Sepakkam, said, 'Lorries transporting the fly ash from the pond are a huge menace. The roads [built on the flood plains] are unstable and they have even caused fatal accidents.

But the biggest problem is from the ash that flies away from the lorry. Everything in our home has ash. We can't even dry our clothes outside.' The village has no access to clean water, Jayanthi has to buy cans of mineral water to drink and everywhere around her is just fly ash. A grey-coloured poison filling up the land, water and air.

Samples collected from this part of the river were more contaminated than even legally allowed levels for treated effluents. Not just water, but even fish, prawns, oysters and crabs from the Ennore Creek contain toxins. Oysters, for instance, were found to have lead—which can harm the bones and the mental development of children—along with selenium and cadmium. Even home-grown vegetables had chromium and lead.

A three-member panel headed by Retd Justice D. Hariparanthaman, assisted by Retd Prof S Janakarajan and Prof Karen Coelho from the Madras Institute of Development Studies, has also said that the pollution around the Ennore area led to the flooding of villages near the river in 2015.[77] At a press conference on the findings of the panel, organised by the Ennore Anaithu Meenava Graama Koottamaippu (Confederation of All the Fishing Villages of Ennore) Hariparanthanam said, 'In Ennore, I saw the [Kosasthalaiyar] river dying a death by a thousand cuts. No development can be worth this kind of destruction.'[78] In recent times, actor-turned-politician Kamal Haasan has lent his celebrity status to the cause of the Ennore Creek as has singer T.M. Krishna, who sang a song in Carnatic style about the need to save poromboke lands, in a song titled, *Chennai Poromboke Paadal*, which was filmed around the creek. The song, written by Kaber Vasuki, and conceptualised by Jayaraman, is a lament on the state of the Ennore and all the ash it is now home to, and seeks to educate people on what poromboke means and why it is important for us to wake up and act now. The word is now used pejoratively.

The song, originally in Tamil and translated to English by Aniruddhan Vasudevan and Karen Coelho, and featured on the Chennai-based Vettiver Collective's YouTube page, provokes with questions.

> The flood has come and gone, what have we learnt from that?
> To construct buildings inside waterbodies, what wisdom is that?
> On the path that rainwater takes to the sea
> What need have we of concrete buildings?
> It was not the rivers that chose to flow through cities
> Rather, it was around rivers that the cities chose to grow
> And lakes that rainwater awaited
> Poromboke—they were reverently labelled

Rowing Against the Tide

During the December floods, Murugan from Kasimedu, a fishing hamlet, had to hold on to electric poles as he rowed his catamaran in the distant Ramapuram area. He described the cries he heard from people inside their homes as something he had never heard before, not since he saw the movie *Titanic* anyway. Despite being a fisherman, he was worried about the water in a few places; it was that dangerous. Murugan, Magesh and others from Kasimedu alone rescued over 500 people in December. This fishing hamlet offered forty boats for rescue work, with everybody in the hamlet forgoing hours of work for free service. They brought all their boats from the sea into the city in trucks.

The 'Covelong Boys', from a surfing school consisting of young men from the fishing community in Kovalam village—now a surfing hub near Chennai—led by Murthy Megavan, used kayaks, fishing boats and catamarans to save 200 girls from a hostel.[79]

The fishing community acted as the first responders during these floods, especially on 2 December, even as rescue teams were struggling to reach a sinking Chennai. This, despite the fishermen having faced a bad experience in November.

During the November floods, a collective of fishermen from the Kottivakkam hamlet, of their own accord, had reached one of the worst hit areas of Chennai, Mudichur, with four boats and rescued around 500 people in one day, giving up that day's work. They set out as early as 6 a.m. to move people to safety. Nanjil Ravi and forty-five others from Kasimedu brought over sixteen fibre boats into the worst-hit areas—Mudichur, Tambaram and Kundrathur. Many of their expensive boats were damaged badly in transit, and some even had large holes at the bottom. They later sought help from the government to repair these boats but had to wait for a long time to get them back in order. Only for the flood to return and for them to rush back to those old places, and many new ones, to rescue more people, risking their own lives and livelihoods further.

When the city corporation requested help from the fishermen in December, R.L. Srinivasan of Kaattukuppam coordinated with other villages in the Ennore area, and with 100 boats, he and others from his community rescued over 30,000 people. 'Our own homes were flooded in Ennore. We moved our people to safety and then went out to rescue others,' Srinivasan said. 'We found rescuing here not as tough as in the other parts because we had the boats here and our people aren't scared of the water.'

Even young children from Ennore were out on the streets with smaller catamarans, helping people to cross flooded roads, Srinivasan said. 'Once we went to the severely flooded parts of the city, we couldn't even think of coming back home. There was no connectivity. People, even those with infants, were trying to walk in that water to get to safety, and we took care of them. There was a home, with twenty children stuck on the top floor. Four of us rescued the children and then very slowly and patiently brought them to safety because we didn't want the kids to feel scared or the boat to wobble. One of us walked in the floodwater to guide the boat in the right direction while others ensured it was moving without any trouble. All along, it was drizzling too.'

In one neighbourhood, Srinivasan and his friends rescued a new mother of twins and took her to safety with great care.

'There was water everywhere and no one had any to drink,' Srinivasan said, echoing that timeless Coleridge poem. 'We took drinking water to a lot of people. We also had food packed with us from volunteers and NGOs and delivered these for hours on end. We didn't take a break to eat though. None of our boys did.'

He too said that many boats were damaged during rescue work, as they hit boulders, fencing, name boards and road dividers. After the waters receded, many boats were left behind on the roads of South Chennai, and the fishermen found it hard to get lorries to transport them back. As a result, the fishing community in Chennai lost up to ten days of work and income. 'We didn't expect anything in return while doing this. During the tsunami, a lot of people came and helped us,' Srinivasan said.

The fishermen's rescue operations during both November and December 2015 were invaluable, and this has to be seen in the light of the fact that boat repairs cost a lot. Though they were given modest emoluments for their work, they did not receive any money for the damage their boats had suffered. They could not take these boats into the sea to fish. As a result, they had to take loans for repair, and work twice or thrice as much as they would otherwise have, to repay the loans. It was, and is, a vicious circle. Banks do not lend to fisherfolk, who end up relying on pawnbrokers, pledging whatever they may have—gold or collaterals—and usually pay high interest rates to loan sharks and private banks.

'Our request for a government-aided cooperative bank with special funding for fisheries, like the ones set up for agricultural purposes, is long pending,' Srinivasan said. In the 1980s and 1990s, the government offered loans to some fisherfolk, and many of them haven't been able to repay it yet. 'It's an extremely small amount and if the government wishes, it can write off those loans in no time. But it has not been done because they don't want people coming back for new loans. Is it not routine for the government to write off agricultural loans and offer new ones? The government doesn't make any investment in the fishing sector.'

Srinivasan also calls on the government to give in-shore fishermen the same kind of importance it gives to deep sea fishermen. 'Some traditional fishermen are involved in deep-sea fishing, but mostly, these are controlled by large firms. They are given up to ₹40 lakh of subsidies per boat. And the government is now allocating ₹200 crore funding to develop tuna fishing, but those firms only create employees, while we are self-reliant.' The TN government announced a plan for the setting up of a 'world-class tuna-fishing harbour' in Thiruvottiyur Kuppam in May 2015. 'We are self-employed and the government thinks long and hard about giving us ₹1 lakh, or boats, engines and nets for us to work. Perhaps the government is worried that if they fund small in-shore fishermen instead of investing in these harbours, we will do well and ask tough questions of them.'

The people of North Chennai, where Srinivasan is from, remained marooned in the floods, their homes filled with water even after the rest of the city had moved on. Srinivasan said that they saw images of South Chennai being flooded on TV and how the people there were affected, while water didn't leave their homes even after it had receded in the rest of the city.

'If there was no North Chennai, Thiruvallur district would have submerged entirely. The mouth of the river, from where it drains, is in North Chennai. Even the media didn't speak about how we were flooded. Maybe they thought it wasn't news that we were drowning. To them it must have been, "So what if these guys drown?" Maybe they don't think of us as equals,' he said. 'We don't think of anyone like that. We treat everyone as our equals. As humans. That's why we went out to help.'

Memories of B'Canal[80]

The Buckingham Canal, or B'Canal as the PWD calls it, runs entirely along the eastern coast of the erstwhile Madras Presidency. It goes from Madras to Mercanum in the south for 106 kms and Madras to Pedda Ganjam in the north for 314 kms. From there it is connected to the deltas of the Krishna and Godavari Rivers. Almost everything has changed now, Madras Presidency is four different states, the city of Madras is Chennai, Merkanam is Marakkanam, and the Buckingham Canal is no longer part tidal, part freshwater. It is all sewage.

Walk back in time, and you'll see a different Buckingham Canal. A hub of commerce, with fish and salt being the locals' prized possessions. At first, called Cochrane's Canal, it was later named after Robert Clive and then finally called Buckingham.

~

It is the glory days of the 1800s. The boats and catamarans on the Buckingham Canal and the boatmen with their long wooden poles have turned Madras into a vision akin to Venice with its famous gondoliers, as stars twinkle high above and the waters glisten. So do the boats, with lights that have been mandated because of all the boat traffic that it witnesses day and night.

Flat bottom steam boats glow with three lights, a white light that is way up there over nine-feet high, right in the middle of the boat. A bull's eye bright red light on the port side and another in green on the starboard side, both of which glimmer at over four feet.

Passenger boats twinkle with lights in each of their cabins, as owlets call out in the distance. Here, in this canal, as twilight strikes, you can hear the groans and grunts of the ashy swallow shrike, the beautiful call of the koel, the shrill vacant happiness of parrots, and the playful rumbling of black-rumped flamebacks, as they all head home having witnessed a sunset that turns the entire place a turmeric hue, like the faces of the city's beautiful women.

On the canal, you see cabin boats, top boats and even barges. On these, you can travel amid mangroves rich in nuts, tamarind and mangoes, and rest in luxurious travellers' bungalows. The people of Nellore and Madras—businessmen, students studying in Pattanam, families scattered between the two places—and their goods traverse up and down the canal regularly, as this is the only means of transport connecting the two big towns.

As we move forward in time to the latter part of the nineteenth century, we can see over 70,000 tons of firewood make its way to Madras, through the canal. The wood is coming in from the island of Sriharikota—from where rockets would be launched into space in the future—and from places north of Madras. All along Madras's Marina and George Town, Indo Saracenic splendours, with their exposed bricks and stained glass, glisten like jewels on the crown, do you see? As these are being built, Madras, larger then than future South India, is like a hungry, wood-loving giant that has to be fed an endless supply of firewood. The exposed bricks that the architect Robert Chisolm so loved, needed to be extra durable. And so this Madras is burning up a lot of wood, from trees of the forests near and far—for bricks, as well as locomotives, mills and the railways—all of which are transported on the Buckingham alongside other goods, worth about ₹100 lakh, collectively. Salt, foodgrains of various kinds and shells for burning lime are also on the canal's boats.[81]

~

The southern Indian coast is deadly for the poor. It is here that the giant killer waves of the tsunami would kill hundreds two centuries later, not to forget the many devastating cyclones and our fishermen being shot or captured at international borders while out in their boats. Though, it is also the bestower of bounty. The coast giveth and the coast taketh away.

The Buckingham Canal on the eastern coast is inextricably linked to that woeful part of Madras's story when millions were left to die on the roads, by the locals as well as the British.

~

It is 1878. As part of the Great Famine of Madras's relief work, on the backs of these people who have been most struck by the famine, a link canal between the Adyar and Cooum Rivers is being built. Soon enough, rice comes into town from the fertile Godavari region through this canal, though most of it does not reach those who are helping build it.

This same year, another part of the Buckingham Canal, between Madras and Bezwada, is being dug in exchange for wages, by what remains of the starving oppressed populace of the Presidency, belonging to the Madiga caste, all of who are on the verge of falling prey to the Great Famine. John Clough, an American Baptist minister—born and raised in New York and Iowa, called 'thatha' or grandpa by the locals, as his hair has turned grey even at forty—oversees the employment of the Madigas, staving off starvation perhaps for thousands. Clough has built palm-leaf huts in the Razupalem village where the poor from far and wide reached in search of work.

Under the harsh sun, as the workers dig the canal, stories of a hero, Jesus, is in the air, acting both as a distraction from the hard labour as well as driving home the message that Christ loved all people equally, even the poor and those despised by others. Thirty staff members from Clough's church are on the site, even as the labourers toil and take turns to travel home to feed their families and come back for more work. Each of the staff is assigned a hundred workers to take care of, and they all soon become well-acquainted. The really weak are offered food, or money for food. Only then come the stories, for Clough does not want to preach to the hungry. He has made it his mission while in India to work with the 'outcast', much to the ire of 'upper caste' Christians. He has also not restricted the Madiga people from following their own culture or mingling with those from their family who continue idol worship.

On the banks of the Gundlakamma River—which once carried Buddhist pilgrims to glorious sites, stupas and monasteries in places like Chandavaram, Dupadu, Pedaganjam, Kanuparti and Uppugundur in Andhra Pradesh—on 3 July 1878, after a good harvest season and the end of the famine, 2,222 of those Clough helped are baptised. And in a matter of three weeks, 9,666 of those he supported (and refused to baptise during the famine, as he thought it would be wrong) have professed their faith in Christianity. The construction of the Buckingham Canal has made Ongole, a district in Andhra Pradesh, the strongest of the denomination in the world this year. Thirty years later, Clough would leave behind a 60,000-strong church.[82]

At last, the historic canal too would see its downfall eventually, like all the water bodies of Madras. As early as 1938, C.W. Ranson, in his book *A City in Transition: Studies in the Social Life of Madras*, said:

> The site of Madras city is very low and very level. The greater part of its surface is alluvial and at no point does it rise more than twenty-five feet above sea-level. The Buckingham Canal is an odorous channel running from the Krishna River. ... Its importance has diminished with the development of railway transport, but it is still used extensively for the carrying of firewood to Madras from the Casuarina plantations to the north and south of the city. As the canal is very shallow (the usual depth of water is from 2 and a half feet to feet 3 and a half feet) the boats are necessarily small and cargoes light.

Beyond Redemption

Today, the Buckingham Canal winding through Chennai and beyond is in a state much worse than Ranson had approved of. Its width has narrowed significantly, from a hundred metres to a mere thirty, because of encroachments and the deposit of huge amounts of silt. It often stinks, as it carries foam-like effluents from sewage treatment plants, and is covered in misleadingly innocent looking beds of water-hyacinth plants, which stop the flow of 'water'. As if these ignominies are not enough, the MRTS trains that connect the northern part of the city to its newer suburb, Velachery, is built on its banks.

The canal receives excess waters from the three main rivers of Chennai, as well as many other drains, cutting through all of them, and is an important part of the city's flood-mitigating arsenal.

Reports of the CAG in 2014, which seem to have been ignored, stressed on the importance of a shortcut diversion from the Okkiyum Maduvu water channel (which is only 1.7 kms away from the sea) via the south Buckingham Canal in Sholinganallur. This shortcut was envisaged as early as 2009 under the Jawaharlal Nehru National Urban Renewal Mission (JNNURM) 'to improve micro drainages in Chennai as part of flood alleviation programme.' If followed, this would have helped drain at least 3500 cusecs of water into the sea, and in effect, the southern part of Chennai could have, would have, should have, not been flooded.

In December 2015, as the Buckingham was already under stress thanks to the Adyar's flooding, the water that drained into it from Okkiyum, did so very slowly, flooding the neighbourhoods around it, claiming its old pathways—from back when it was more than three times wider—and lives.

Flood mitigation remains but a distant dream for several parts of Chennai, despite the crores spent on it. Only in March 2019, ahead of the announcement of general elections, did the TN government announce that it was going to build new canals for flood management. The budgetary allocation for irrigation and flood control for the year 2019–20 is ₹5.071 crore, a 38 per cent increase from the previous year.

Conservationists and environmentalists now fear that we may never be able to recover the canal that has been blocked in several places, in order to allow floodwaters to pass through freely. The state seems to be on war with these water bodies. Some argue that the state has deliberately pushed the water ecosystem into such a bad condition that covering them up to build shiny concrete structures will no longer seem like a bad idea to its inhabitants. After all, who wants mosquito- and stench-ridden stretches winding through their posh new suburbs?

'The Rains Still Make Me Nervous'

Twenty-eight-year-old Rufus John Samuel has been a Chennai-vasi all his life. His family lived in Tondiarpet in the north of the city for a few years, before moving to Ekkaduthangal in the south in 1993. Ekkaduthangal, a busy part of town near the airport and on the banks of the Adyar, across from West Saidapet, has grown from a hub for small and medium industries into a bustling neighbourhood with star hotels and tech parks over the last decade. Samuel's family has been living here for over two decades now. His maternal grandmother and her family continue to stay in North Chennai while his family moved to be closer to his father's workplace. His mother, now a homemaker, was earlier working in a non-teaching position in a college, while his father works in a private firm in Gopalapuram and travels a lot around the country.

Heavy showers were walloping parts of the city, all through the night of 1 December. Samuel remembers it being like any other evening, apart from the rains outside, that is. He had a late dinner, was checking social media for updates and even as late as 1.30 a.m., his air-conditioning was on. In the wee hours of the morning, some time between 4.30 and 5 a.m., a power shutdown woke him up. What a day it would turn out to be.

Samuel recalled his mother telling him that 'water', that misnomer all of us used that month for what entered our homes, had reached the next street. She insisted he go and see what was happening. There was panic in her voice.

'You know how mothers are, they anticipate the worst and prepare for it ahead, right?' he asked me when I interviewed him for the book. I had to agree with him on that.

~

The worst did indeed come true, for someone else. Around the same time that Samuel was comforting his mother, seventy-two-year-old retired Lt Col G. Venkatesan, and his sixty-year-old wife V. Geetha, were crying for help a little away from Samuel's house. Their ground-floor house, which didn't even have a staircase leading to the terrace, was going under. As the pool of destruction invaded their house in Defence Colony, they struggled and screamed aloud for help. The couple was not able to locate the house keys. It had been displaced by the river that had snuck into their home in the dead of the night. Neighbours heard them, both husband and wife, call for help, over a period of nine hours, but could not do anything. They were utterly helpless. Neither the navy's inflatable boat nor the local fishermen's fibre boat could handle the Adyar in spate. No one came to take them away. Just as no one had come to warn them ahead.

The two of them would first stand on the table in their bedroom and shout for help. Later, they would add a chair to the top of the table and sit on it. All along they would be on the phone, talking to their daughter, telling her where the water was. Ankle. Hip. Neck ...

And then the cries would die. So would they. Water would rise to ten feet inside the house. A rescue team would show up on 3 December, one day after what should have been Geetha's sixtieth birthday.[83]

~

In Samuel's house, he was trying to pacify his mother by pointing out that their street was a bit higher than the others in the area and so the flood couldn't possibly hit them. That didn't comfort her, she wanted to be sure. She wanted to put things away to safety. Samuel still felt complacent about going out at that time of the morning to see what was happening.

'I had this stubborn bravado of sorts, then. I thought, there's no way our home would flood,' he told me, a wry smile appearing on his face as he thought back to that morning.

At last, when he finally shook off whatever was holding him back and went out, he saw a lot of people walking on the streets, an unusual number for that hour.

'People were going as if to see some thiruvizha [carnival]. At that time, for everyone it was just some entertainment, right? "Oh, one entire street has filled up, cars are half-submerged and the water is slowly moving. Our street hasn't, let's go see."'

The people out and about were convinced that the river wouldn't cross their street because subsequent streets would have to submerge before the water reached theirs, for which a lot of water would have had to be let out.

'Government would have warned us, no, if they were sending out so much water?' the people were convincing themselves.

'There was no warning. Not even an announcement asking us to be careful. If nothing else, people would have put away things to safety, right?' Samuel told me.

He returned home and told his mother, 'Amma, don't worry. There's water in the next street but it's only lapping now. Not furious. It won't come here.'

Still, they disconnected all the appliances at home and had a quick, basic breakfast. By the time they finished breakfast and started to pack up the things in their home, the neighbours were at their door.

'It's crossed the next street and has started coming into ours. It's time to do something drastic,' they said.

Samuel's house is on the ground floor in a building with three other apartments. That morning in his home, there was Samuel, his parents and grandmother. As his street was being taken over by the Adyar, he walked again to the main road, Jawaharlal Nehru Salai, to see what was happening. When he reached there, he realised just how serious things were. He called work to let them know he won't be coming in. He heard that his workplace in Sholinganallur was inundated too. He messaged his friends and aunt that water was beginning to close in on their home. That was the last bit of information to go out from his family. After that, it would be two or three days before anyone would even hear from them. The phone network would die. The previous evening, Samuel had charged his phone and had readied a power bank.

'In hindsight, I realise there's no point to all that because what can one do with 100 per cent power in their phone when there's no signal? Throughout the flood, my phone had power but I could reach no one.'

By around 9 in the morning, water had reached their home. The level was rising slowly, though.

'I don't have any pictures to show you. I was too busy moving things. It didn't strike me then to take pictures.'

The neighbours came together and helped each other out. Samuel helped load whatever he possibly could on top of the bed in his neighbour's house and put away documents in the highest possible place in the house. Then he came back to his home and repeated the task with the neighbours' help.

'Our home has those old school electricity boards, not the new digital ones. At that time of the morning, for a while, the power kept coming and going. Suddenly we'd see a spark somewhere.' And that's when they heard that the water was going to fill up their homes too and that they had to evacuate. Panic had set in in the neighbourhood and dark rumours began to swirl.

'People were saying the water will reach twenty feet, by night it will reach the second floor. That Defence Colony is entirely flooded and few families have died already.'

Gas cylinders were floating like balloons inside his home soon enough. Samuel tried to carry the LPG cylinder, while the old EB board sparked every now and then.

'It was a really scary couple of seconds for me as I carried it away to safety,' he said. 'We had great neighbours on the first floor, who put up with us for two days. Me, my paatima, amma and appa. They cooked for us too. They had stocked up on some ready-to-eat foods but they were a big family as well. Soon enough, we ran out of fresh water.'

The first day no one dared to venture out. Through the night, the young in the building took turns to see where the water had reached, by the torchlights on their phones. The EB board became the gauge to check whether the level of the water was going up or down.

'Somehow, even though the drainage system in our area is messy, after a day and a half, the water started to recede.'

Soon, it receded enough for him to venture out. 'That's when the scale of what had happened hit me. My father was sure they had let out the waters somewhere. There was no way that the rainwater was causing this. Mother Nature is cruel but this was not just that.'

Milk and drinking water had become expensive, he learnt, as he walked along the slushy streets with animal carcasses floating everywhere he looked. A regular bottle of fresh water was ₹400. Half-a-litre milk, ₹200.

Samuel walked to the main road and saw that it had been cordoned off. Water was raging under the bridge and the debris from the deluge had appropriated the sides of the road. Dead cows and all kinds of animals, crawling insects, snakes, luxury cars were floating around. The roads looked a picture of disaster.

'I don't know how many people were bitten by poisonous insects,' Samuel said. Things were so bad that the city municipal corporation's staff were on the roads, prodding 'things' in the debris to see if it was alive. Samuel saw a corpse floating nearby and heard one of the staff members ask, 'He's wearing a blue shirt. Does anyone recognise this man?'

Jaya TV's office on that road had gone under water. As had Puthiya Thalaimurai's across the road and Vendhar TV's. All three channels had to suspend their services temporarily.

'We started rationing food because in the stores accessible to us, they were running out of supplies,' Samuel said. Later in the day, the helicopters with aid began hovering over their street. People went to the tallest house in the neighbourhood, where rations were dropped off, and brought back home what they could—bread, jam and water.

The moment the water receded, the family left to Samuel's grandmother's house in Thiruvottiyur.

'Nobody wanted to touch Ekkaduthangal during the rescue operations. I am not sure why. No one came to where we lived during the floods on a boat, asking us to leave or taking us away to a safe place. I still haven't understood why this happened. I cannot bring myself to watch anything about this again. There was a documentary on this on the National Geographic. I want to watch it, but I don't feel like it.'

More than the trauma of the flood, it was the aftermath that hit him hard.

'You walk into the home you've lived in for most of your life and you see the damage that nature has unleashed on you, it kind of puts things in perspective. That was my biggest takeaway from this.'

Samuel and his family washed down the entire house. All the wood in the house was bloated and they couldn't lock the door for days. Photographs collected over years, memories of vacations from years ago and his parents' wedding album were damaged in the rains. Everything in the house made from plywood was as good as dead. Books, music systems, old cassettes and CDs of gospel music and some old classics, electronics ... all gone.

For a while after the flood, the family wasn't sure if the water in the borewell was safe for use, and relied on store-bought water for everything. The groundwater was sent to a lab before they went back to using it. Shuttling between Ekkaduthangal and Thiruvottiyur on a daily basis with mugs and buckets, the family cleaned the house every day over a week.

'The rains still make me nervous,' Samuel said. When people post on their social media accounts about rains in Chennai, with a sense of relief during hot days, he no longer knows how to react.

'We do know how much people lost in these floods, and how much worse it was for others. Thankfully, we were able to bear our cross. We came out okay.'

Like the Smell of Drying Fish ...

... that lie, their silvery bodies gleaming, on the hot, brown sands of our beaches, rumours spread from street to street, home to home, device to device. Striking fear in the hearts of our people. All through this flood fiasco.

Here's a thing I learned during the floods. Some people are naive. Some are fools. Some are just cruel. The coming together of these three, especially during disasters, is heartbreaking and infuriating all at once. Call it misinformation, post-truth, whatever, but the deliberate lying on mass media and the disclaimer 'Forwarded as received' is a punishing joke. This became apparent as soon as the rains began. Though, to be fair, some lies were as old as 1985. People love lying, don't they?

Back in 1985, when Chennai flooded, there were rumours that crocodiles had escaped the Madras Crocodile Bank Trust (Croc Bank). And since we steadfastly refuse to learn from history, we are doomed, here in Chennai, to this *Groundhog Day*-like charade of repetition. This rumour came back with a vengeance in November and December 2015. It began around 25 November and the Croc Bank had to repeatedly put out messages to stop false information spreading like wildfire, every day, with increasing vigour. Their official Twitter handle first tried to bust the hoax on 25 November, then 2 December, then 4 and 7 December.

On 4 December, their tweet read:

> The rumours are still "floating" we see … We are not compromised. No crocodiles have escaped from our facility. No walls have broken. We are doing the best we can to ensure that none of this happens. All precautionary measures are being taken. Well just to reiterate once again we are not sure where or how this started but we would certainly like to meet the person who started it all. Most certainly the news channels which reported this. We'll get back to that when this phase is over. Enough with the rumours already. Please.

The rumours eventually even made it to the newspapers, with the Tamil daily *Dinamalar*'s e-portal carrying a photo of a crocodile, from Vadodara's streets originally, on 6 December, with just a caption: 'Crocodile on the Road? (*Saalaiyil mudhalai nadamaatam?*)'. There were also rumours that animals from the Vandalur Zoo had escaped. Though it was true that the zoo had gone under water and a wall had broken, officials reassured news organisations repeatedly that no animal had escaped.

Earlier in December, our WhatsApp and SMS folders received a disgraceful message, made further uncouth by an unnecessary number of exclamation points, as if the lies would somehow turn into truth if those phallic displays, as Elena Ferrante calls them, were used repeatedly. If F. Scott Fitzgerald were here now, he would have possibly said, an exclamation point is like believing your own WhatsApp rumour.

The message we received read like this:

> Guys CHENNAI IS ON HIGH ALERT NOW!!! NASA has warned INDIA tat CHENNAI will suffer ah very very high rainfall with a hurricane !!! NASA has given 2 dates 21,22 ...on these 2 days unpredictable rainfall in the history of INDIA will lash tamilnadu ... the rainfall will be about 250 cm in CHENNAI!!! So indian central gov has now deployed 3000 NDRF to tamilnadu and border security force and airforce and army on the toes ....!! NASA's prediction never miss ....! Watch CNN IBN they r telecasting the live show ....!!

There was no such show on CNN IBN.

Here is another gem that made the rounds around 7 December.

> Warning:
> if any of your friends or relatives are living in Chennai ask them to leave Chennai immediately because in the next 72 hours very heavy rain is expected more than multiple level of the present rain. As per NASA Report this is not the ordinary rain. It's name is EL Nino cyclone. There is a chance for 250 cm rain. Chances are there nearly the entire Chennai may be submerged in water. Search in Google, you will understand. Somehow inform of your friends and relatives in Chennai ....
>
> Wipro announces to drop people to out of Chennai city. Over 100 wipro buses starts tomorrow 7 am - 8.30am from Koyambedu bus stop. Please share this message to those stuck in Chennai.....
>
> Spread the news tomorrow 6 flights gonna take off from Arakkonam air base. Flat rates of 1000 rs for any city in south India and 2000 for north India . Only hand baggage allowed

> Air India flights to Hyderabad for ₹1000 and Delhi For ₹2000 only for emergency cases
>
> Pls post this to diff.groups

Who benefits from lies spread on social media? What can they possibly achieve by spreading panic? I haven't found the answers to these questions yet, but then, these too are human traits. Much the way the city and its people rose to the occasion (ah, I hate this phrase but do we have a choice?), there were some revelling in the—mischief is too mild a word—havoc they were wreaking on an already grieving, hurt, trapped people.

The hysteria that follows such rumour-mongering at times of disasters can have serious implications. There is a need for everyone getting on social media, and those around them, to find out if the information they receive is reliable or not. But at times of disaster, with limited connectivity, fact-checking is not always possible. 'Better safe than sorry' is running through all our minds, but really, what safety can be achieved by spreading information that can only strike fear in people's hearts? How can people escape crocodiles, while stuck in neck-deep water?

On the morning of 4 December, after the waters had subsided, some of us were out volunteering, distributing hot food packets. This was us paying it forward. Many who volunteered during the floods were those who themselves had been trapped and had been at the receiving end of the generosity of strangers, random acts of kindness, and volunteers distributing food and water. My parents were among them. When my father said, 'For the first time in my life, I realised what it felt like to stand in a sort-of queue and receive food from some volunteer and a case of water bottles,' it hit us all hard. My parents had run out of drinking water and by the last day, out of food. We knew we had to do this for others. And thousands others felt the same way.

And so, with over 500 packets of hot sambar rice, sanitary napkins, diapers, water bottles and emergency medicines, we reached Rangarajapuram. The food disappeared in no time as residents scrambled for it, and we fell short. They requested dinner as well, and 1,000 packets this time.

What we did not know then was that that very afternoon, someone sitting somewhere with a not-so-smartphone had put out a message on social media that the Chembarambakkam Reservoir had burst open and that the entire city would soon be submerged. This rumour, of course, like rumours tend to do, reached Rangarajapuram. When we went back that night with the 1,000 packets of hot food, the entire neighbourhood was empty—almost 300 families had fled in utter panic and chaos leaving everything behind. It looked as if they were out to start a new life elsewhere. Doors were open, things were strewn along the street and homes lay abandoned. No one knew where they had gone. The few people who had stayed back asked us, each one of us, if this rumour was true. Including an old woman who had waited for her son to come and take her away during the two excruciating days of flooding.

Since we still had a lot of food (two cars packed to the gills) and wanted to reach people who were really in need, we went to a police station in the nearby Kotturpuram area and asked them where we could go. Raj Kumar, from the station, got on a bike even as it started to pour on the way, and guided us deep into the neighbourhood, to a place where aid and relief never reached. 'They don't get anything because no one cares,' he said.

We offloaded food for 148 families at the Kuruvikkaaran colony, along with water, mosquito coils and other necessities. The colony is home to the marginalised narikurava community.[84] Raj Kumar, who knew everyone in the colony, contacted the 'thalaivar' of the community and had him come and speak to us and collect the necessaries, so it could reach every single family.

It was a similar story in Ashok Nagar. When the Chembarambakkam breach rumour reached the people on 4 December at around 4 p.m., hundreds of families fled to 'safety', to the metro station. The same story repeated itself in Polichalur, where too people fled their homes following that very rumour. Just the previous day, on 3 December, rumours had floated in believable meme formats with a photograph to boot, that the cricket stadium in Chepauk had been opened up for the needy (or 'needies!!' as the post claimed).

Lake, reservoir and river breach warnings kept doing the rounds through the month. First, it was warnings about flooding in the Keezhkattalai, then Porur, later Kelambakkam, and then Chembarambakkam areas. Then came the ones about Adyar, Porur, Irumbuliyur, Potheri and then between Thaiyur and Thiruporur neighbourhoods. Later, there was one that claimed that the Kotturpuram Bridge had collapsed as the Adyar River overflowed. Round and round these messages went. Some rumours were so strong that they reached out-of-towners, who then sent them to more locals, who, believing these out-of-towners, left Chennai, abandoning their homes.

Chennai's IT Corridor, which saw heavy flooding, shut shop for a while, as it went under water. Close to 80,000 people had not reported back to work as late as 12 December 2015, as rumours flew thick and fast about breaches and covered-up deaths inside the IT parks.

A serious allegation was levelled against DLF Cybercity, spread across 44.4 acres on Old Mahabalipuram Road. Over fifty companies have their offices in this IT park, located in a Special Economic Zone area in Nandambakkam, which saw some of the worst flooding in the city. Social media was filled with messages that several people were possibly trapped or worse, dead in the basement.

The Tamil weekly *Vikatan* ran a long story on the heavy-duty bundobast including security personnel and police around the building, who were hostile to locals as wells as reporters, and said that people were suspicious about the way DLF was handling the issue.

Several employees left town and others moved to company branches in different cities to continue work, but activity seemed to increase inside DLF. As the public was cordoned off, questions like, 'What are they trying to hide?' began to do the rounds, even in the media. Soon, the police got involved. On 12 December, the Chennai police issued a statement to clarify that upon inspection of the campus, no bodies were found to be floating around the basement, though several hundred cars were. A spokesperson for the company, in a statement to the press, said that he believed the employees were spreading such rumours, in their avarice to claim the vehicles they had parked in the basement of the IT Park on the day of the floods. The entire basement, which could fit 5,000 cars, and was 22 acres and 12 metres deep, had filled up with water, and the company used 60 pumps to drain it.

On 11 December, a fact-finding team from Knowledge Professionals Forum, a hierarchy-less collective 'of IT professionals working together for society, gender equality and openness in IT industry', published a report that put these speculations to rest. On 14 December, Forum for IT Employees, another collective of IT professionals, too put out a report to clarify the truth, although it continued to express scepticism about the sketchy answers and the rude outlook of the IT park's personnel. The forum also expressed concern for the non-Tamil-speaking staff who may have been stuck in the basement and gone missing. 'We at F.I.T.E at this point of time shall say that truth cannot be hidden for a longer period of time and will anyway find its way out eventually,' its statement read.

The lines between fact and fiction were fluid when we were under siege. Misinformation, alternative facts, especially in times of calamity, spread like a plague of locusts.

With the public and media participating in this charade, could politicians be far?

Higher than the stench of the Cooum, was the stink raised by the shenanigans of our elected representatives. As people from all over the country contributed towards relief and rehabilitation of the affected, and trucks and vehicles filled with aid made their way to the needy on 4 December, social media was inundated with photographs of workers of the ruling AIADMK party forcing volunteers to add stickers that had Amma's face. Many volunteers who were distributing aid complained on Twitter and Facebook with photographic evidence that they were being threatened to add these stickers, which would make it look like the ruling party and, in effect, the government, was giving out aid, while in reality, it was the result of spontaneous, philanthropic outbursts of everyday people. The opposition party, Dravida Munnetra Kazhagam (DMK), posted pictures of this sticker fiasco and called it 'a disgraceful act'. The ruling party, in turn, called this a lie and issued a statement that all this was being done to defame them, adding to the tangle of lies and counter-lies. Newspapers reported that following this incident, and given the inadequacy of the government's relief measures, ministers were heckled in the then chief minister Jayalalithaa's constituency, RK Nagar.

A photo of Prime Minister Narendra Modi surveying the floods from a helicopter was shoddily photoshopped. By the Press Information Bureau (PIB). Yes. The official media organ of the Centre. In this photograph, Modi was looking out the window of an aircraft, and the 'view' was clearly morphed to show an image of flooded Chennai. The PIB tweeted this photo with the caption, 'PM @narendramodi conducting aerial survey of rain hit area in Tamil Nadu'. Following severe criticism, the PIB took the tweet down. The following day it issued a clarification. The statement read:

> Pictures of Hon'ble Prime Minister, Shri Narendra Modi undertaking the aerial survey of flood-affected areas of Tamil Nadu were released on PIB Twitter Handle and PIB's website last evening. Out of the seven pictures released, one picture used the technique of merging two pictures. This is being referred to as "Photoshopping" in sections of media. This happened due to error of judgement and the picture was subsequently deleted. PIB regrets the release of the above mentioned picture. Inconvenience caused is regretted.

Journalist Rahul M tweeted on 3 April 2018 that he had filed 'an RTI seeking clarification about the manipulated image of Modi inspecting Chennai during floods' in 2015. The Information and Broadcasting Ministry of India responded to his query thus: 'Merging two photographs of Hon'ble Prime Minister Shri Narendra Modi has been done as per previous standard practice.'

Soon enough, religious bigotry made its way into this complex network of lie manufacturing. False stories of Christian missionaries distributing Bibles while Hindu organisations were doing charity work, supported by photographs over a year old, were shared by 'anti-conversion' brigades on Twitter, sitting safe and far away from the scene of flooding, no doubt.

Later that week, the TV channel ABP News decried a photograph being attributed to it as being fake. In the said photo, police were seen beating up RSS workers. A message that accompanied the photo claimed that RSS's swayamsevaks, or part-time volunteers, were caught trying to steal jewellery in the guise of helping people during the Chennai floods.

By the time volunteers could battle many of these messages online, the lies, as they tend to, had travelled half-way around the world.

The collective trauma that the flooding and the absolute lack of preparedness of our institutions had inflicted on us that week, were reinforced over and over again, as these rumours found their way into our homes, and we battled fatigue and helplessness.

~

Anantha Narayanan, who had a close shave with the floods and shared his ordeal with me generously for this book, lives on the eighth floor of his building in Keezhkattalai. Just as his sister-in-law Lavanya couldn't access his home despite reaching the neighbourhood, two floors beneath them, the brother of a young man who lived in the building called to tell his family that he was at the Keezhkattalai bus stand and would figure out a way home. The young man's brotherly instincts kicked in just as he heard his sibling's voice on the phone. He decided to go and bring his brother back to safety. His wife asked him not to go, for she knew there was no flooding at the bus stop. The argument escalated, and finally, he told his wife to go into the room as nothing she said would stop him from going to look for his little brother.

'You won't even know that I am gone,' he said and left home.

He walked out the gate, where water wasn't as bad as he thought it would be. But when he reached the intersection, water was flowing ferociously underneath the highway. He used a wall running across for support, as he began to cross over to the other side. People standing by asked him to stay put, but he was insistent. What the young man didn't realise was that the water's force had started to eat into the sides of the road. Even when he reached the end of the wall, he continued to walk thinking that the tar road under his feet would be firm. But there was nothing there. He went into the water.

For about three days, nobody knew where he was. They went looking for him everywhere and finally found him in a mortuary. His wife was kept in the dark. The younger brother, who had made it home safe, went to the mortuary along with his friends and had to identify his brother by his wedding ring. Even then, they didn't tell his wife, until they were absolutely sure it was him and the formalities at the mortuary were complete. Finally, when they told her, she said, 'I don't want to see him. I want to remember him the way I do now.' They were married for only one year. It was a love marriage, against the wishes of both parents.

She handed over his wedding suit to them and told them to complete the formalities.

Two days later, there was a video on Facebook. Someone on the side of a road, on a bike or a car, had seen a body flowing in a canal. They used a couple of logs from a timber mart abutting the canal and pulled it out. They then placed the body on the side of the road. Someone else filmed the whole thing. The camera moved past all the onlookers, into the crowd, and then was placed in front of the body, focussing on his face, for a while.

It had landed on Narayanan's Facebook feed through a common friend's post. He was the first to see it among the people who knew the dead young man. The man who had filmed it was asked to take the video down, and he did. Later, when Narayanan asked the man behind the camera, why he had filmed this, the man told him, 'It was an unidentified body. I thought if I did this someone would figure out who he was.'

Narayanan spoke of humankind's fascination for the morbid and this urge now to record and disseminate everything, which is what led that man to film the whole thing and post it online for all of the world to see.

'He could have easily stopped filming and described the human,' Narayanan told me. 'The wife could have chanced upon this video, right? She hadn't wanted to see him that way.'

Red Rice's Debt

Among the many stories I heard in the course of the three years following the floods, there is one narrative of rescue and relief that the world needs to hear. Especially now, as refugees worldwide face not only uncertainties and untold suffering but also bear the brunt of ignorance and xenophobia.

It is the story of how the Eelam Tamils, who had left their war-torn homeland with nothing in their hands, saved the day, again, as locals sought refuge and rehabilitation during the floods.

The Organisation for Eelam Refugees Rehabilitation (OfERR) is for, of and by Eelam refugees. S.C. Chandrahasan, who was an advocate practising in Sri Lanka, upon arriving in Chennai, got together with a group of educated refugees and locals and set up this organisation in 1984, to enable the community to champion their own rights and work for their community. OfERR works with the TN government, and its success lies in this unique approach. As a result, even the UN Refugee Agency (UNHCR) is not allowed to work in refugee camps in TN, while OfERR is. This is only possible because OfERR is made up of refugees living in those camps.

To understand why Tamil refugees helped thousands of locals during the floods, one must also understand OfERR's journey. I spoke to Poongkothai, Chandrahasan's daughter, about the organisation. A documentary filmmaker, she is currently the director of new programmes at OfERR.

'Initially, when we started, my father asked the government to allow refugees access to the same education that locals have in the government schools, and Kalaignar [the then chief minister M. Karunanidhi] immediately granted that. As a result, we have an educated refugee populace. We had, at one point, over one lakh refugees in TN and now, after the war, it has gone down to 64,000, with people going back,' Poongkothai said. There is 100 per cent literacy and over 4,000 graduates among the Eelam refugee community in Chennai. Over the years, this organisation run by refugees created an infrastructure of a self-reliant community, with trained counsellors, teachers and health and women empowerment workers.

Refugees from Sri Lanka have seen bombings, loved ones' death, rape or their children being taken away as child soldiers. 'There were very high suicide rates initially in the camps as you can imagine,' Poongkothai said. Counsellors from OfeRR played an important role in the psychological and overall well-being of those in the camps.

'The first time we went out and started working with the Indian community was when the tsunami struck in 2004,' Poongkothai said. 'We didn't go in initially with funding. Our people went in, as the tragedy unfolded, with their bare hands, to help locals.' She paused a beat before adding, 'The first thing they did was to help Indians clear the dead bodies. Initially, the refugees helped with what they had with them—their experience.'

The health workers, women and counsellors offered their precious words of solace and services to many who had lost loved ones and homes to the tsunami. 'That was our first intervention.

This time [during the floods], the refugees went out and gave back to the Indian community.'

If you are wondering why the refugees were helping the host community, something unheard of in any refugee situation in the world, here is how Poongkothai explained it: 'It's because the people of Tamil Nadu have embraced the Tamil refugees. Not just the government, it's the people themselves.'

Take Thenmozhi, who is now a women empowerment coordinator at OfERR, has helped set up over 600 SHGs in the camps, of which 400 still remain, and the women have amassed a savings of ₹2 crore. Thenmozhi came as a refugee after the army attacked her town Velanai. The entire populace fled to Delf from where she came across to India with her family in a small fishing boat. She did not land in Rameshwaram, where many of the Sri Lankan refugees end up, but in a small village called Thondi in TN. In Thondi, the locals, despite being impoverished and not having enough clothing for themselves, gave Thenmozhi and her family dry clothes and whatever food they could, like kanji, or porridge.

'This is a story that I have heard over and over again from refugees. The fact that the Tamil people of Tamil Nadu treated them as their own brethren and shared what little they had with them, and for that they have always had a sense of gratitude,' Poongkothai said. This is what brought the Eelam Tamils out of their camps and into the homes of the locals in 2004, when tragedy struck in the form of killer tidal waves. Since refugee camps are spread all over the state, during the tsunami, the refugees, whose camps were closest to the remote areas that were hit, were the first to help in many places.

'My father says it is because of the senjotrukkadan we feel towards the people of Tamil Nadu,' Poongkothai said.

Senjotrukkadan is a unique Tamil phrase that means showing indebtedness to those who have given one food and clothing.Senjoru means red rice and kadan means debt. Red rice's debt. That word and the underlying sentiment has been part of the Tamil consciousness for aeons. It appears in one of the five great Tamil epics, *Seevaka Sinthamani*, composed over a thousand years ago by the Jain monk Thiruthakka Thevar. It was immortalised in a moving song, *Ullathil Nalla Ullam*, penned by poet Kannadasan and sung by Seerkazhi Govindarajan in the 1964 film *Karnan*. The movie extols the virtues of Kunti's most interesting son, played by Sivaji Ganesan. In the Kurukshetra battleground, Karnan fights on the side of his friend Duryodhanan to show him gratitude, for senjotrukkadan, against his own brothers the Pandavas.

By 2004, OfERR's volunteers had been living in refugee camps for over a decade. The temporary housing given to tsunami victims was similar to their own. About 640 Eelam refugees who worked with tsunami victims were able to understand the problems of living in temporary one-room shelters, better than anyone else. OfERR received funding from the European Civil Protection and Humanitarian Aid Operations (ECHO) and the people of Eelam helped build improved housing for victims of the tsunami. They repaired and replaced broken houses and distributed food to nearly 45,000 people.

They worked in sixty to seventy villages in Kanyakumari, Cuddalore and Nagapattinam over a period of ten years, adopting the same model with which they had empowered themselves.

From among the tsunami victims, the Eelam refugees helped train counsellors, health and women empowerment workers, till the TN government stepped in to provide permanent housing.

OfERR, through its relationship with TOMS, USA, also receives over 100,000 shoes every year for its refugee community. 'Our community said they wanted to share this with the locals and they went to nearby schools and took the sizes of all the children. They actually measure 110,000 or 220,000 children in the poorest schools around our refugee villages.' The community has worked with 1000 schools in TN and has distributed a million shoes so far.

By December 2015, OfERR and the refugee community had amassed a lot of experience in working with the locals in need. A large number of those they helped during the floods were poor, living in the most rural, most backward areas. OfERR's office was also badly hit that December, as it is on the roof of a building and is modelled after the temporary housing the refugees have. The staff living in the refugee camps could not come into the office because trains were suspended, and everyone stayed put. But just three days after the flooding, OfERR set up a relief drop-off in Don Bosco school in Chennai.

All of OfERR's volunteers, including refugee girls staying at the girls' hostel, showed up to help. As soon as Poongkothai posted a message on Facebook saying OfERR was collecting relief, lorries upon lorries of relief material started to pour in. Racer Narain Karthikeyan and his wife Pavarna, for instance, sent a truck filled with aid. Shanti and Brahmal Vasudevan, Sri Lankan Tamils who contribute to a revolving fund for the refugees' education, also contributed to OfERR's flood relief fund in Chennai and continue to fund its rural outreach programme.

Twelve-year-old Tara from Dubai was in Chennai during the floods. She interviewed Poongkothai, went back to her school, spoke to her peers and raised about ₹2 lakh, on her own, and sent it back. OfERR's volunteers loaded and unloaded the relief material, and as the waters receded, the more senior staff also joined the relief efforts.

'A lot of our regional volunteers came in. Those who were a part of TOMS distribution were especially helpful because they knew where exactly aid was needed,' Poongkothai said. People from affected villages, once they knew OfERR was involved, began to apply for their own needs as well as their community's. And then, other locals turned up at the venue to volunteer alongside the refugees. These were people from every walk of life—advertising professionals, students and women who manned ironing stalls in street corners—who helped to maintain the registers; to pack, unpack, load and unload food; and to ensure that the food was still fresh and safe to eat by the time it reached the centre. People came in autorickshaws with whatever they had in their refrigerator and shared it at the drop-off point.

'A lot of groups of young people from the city were giving out relief during the floods. But the thing is, one has to have a system, otherwise the more vulnerable people get left out,' Poongkothai said. 'Somebody would go in a car or a truck and they would open up the back of the truck and there would be shoving and pushing. So households who had strong men were able to get in and get the relief.'

That this sensitivity, absent in almost every other relief work organised spontaneously by the locals during the floods, was present in an organisation made of people who had lost everything, much like the people they were helping, is both unsurprising and poignant. At the relief camp, when representatives from the villages or slums visited the office to lay out what their needs were, OfERR's volunteers accompanied them to their community to do a headcount and to make note of the families and their needs—if the family had a baby or elderly people, and so on. Family packs were made keeping in mind these various requirements. Two more volunteers then headed out to distribute tokens. Families with babies got the aid first, then families with the elderly and those with special needs and finally the rest. The trucks filled with aid were also given protection by the Chennai police in a bid to ward off any attempts at ransacking, which were reported in various parts of the city and in the villages.

'I love the fact that a lot of young people were going out and giving aid but I guess they didn't realise that there are many other factors at play and that's where being an NGO comes in handy,' Poongkothai said.

Rather than just stopping with aid for a day or two, OfERR's volunteers continued to follow up until the families were okay. Most families in the Chennai area were rehabilitated under a month. In the far-flung villages, help seemed to be less forthcoming. These included families in thirty villages, with Dalits who did not receive aid. Around Cuddalore and Chidambaram, their houses had not been repaired yet.

OfERR tied up with the Kollywood actors' organisation, Nadigar Sangam, with the help of actor Karthi and others, for the complete rehabilitation of the areas overlooked by others. It set up tuition centres and these became the focal point for the community to come together. It set up children's parliaments, which empowered children to advocate for the community's rights. When administrators and those in power saw children in their offices, carrying letters with the demands of their communities, they became curious and often immediately called the children in to ask what they needed. OfERR learned that the bureaucrats were more receptive to children taking ownership, and it proved to be an effective way to help the local communities. Actor Surya's Agaram foundation helped identify school dropouts, rehabilitated them and offered them scholarships for vocational training.

'Children tend to be more united. It will surprise you to learn how many benefits the villages have received thanks to these children,' Poongkothai said. The tuition centres are headed by graduates from the village, so they are able to continue with their education and join a post-graduation course, while the school kids feel encouraged to go to school. OfERR's volunteers also conduct livelihood workshops—tailoring, jewellery making, candle making, computer education—to help the women in these villages leave behind acute poverty.

All of this is being done by the refugee population in TN. The women empowerment trainer for this project, for instance, is Nagalakshmi. Now forty-nine years old, she arrived in India as a teen and was separated from her mother and father, who had to send her away on a boat to save her life. 'She [Nagalakshmi] says, "I am an orphan," because she hasn't seen her parents and has lived alone all her life in the camp. She has a hut of her own and has no family here,' Poongkothai told me.

Thenmozhi and Poongkothai, along with OfERR's education coordinator, Padmanabhan, held interviews and selected staff from among the villages affected by the floods, and then

Nagalakshmi trained those selected, who in turn went back and trained other women in the villages. Padmanabhan, who too came to India as a young refugee, travelled to far-flung villages to identify their needs and help set up tuition centres.

Amarnath, the coordinator for the Flood Relief Project, later renamed as Rural Development Project, is also a Tamil refugee who came to India when he was very young. Amarnath is a maths graduate, educated in TN. The assistant coordinator for this project is Saravanan, a refugee as well. He is now married and has two kids who were born in the refugee camp.

When a dance school from the USA sent $ 8000 as flood rehabilitation donation, OfERR decided to build toilets for these communities. They put this money to use through a government scheme wherein if a family pools in ₹3,000, the government will pitch in with the remaining amount to build a toilet. These are families for whom ₹3,000 is sometimes all of their monthly income, and they do not have that much to put away for a toilet. The trainers from OfERR also help locals understand hygiene and maintenance of toilets.

As time went on, it became really difficult for OfERR to find funding for the rehabilitation work in villages. 'We have international funding for OfERR because we are an international issue—refugees. But for these rural villages in Tamil Nadu, it's hard to find funds.'

Even corporates, flush with corporate social responsibility (CSR) cash, are only willing to invest in a forty-mile radius of their office, and not in remote areas. So it is mostly the urban poor who benefit from CSR initiatives. Poongkothai also recently set up the Serendip Boutique, a social enterprise that sells products made by women from villages affected by the Chennai floods, which is incubated by the Loyola Institute of Business Administration. The proceeds go back to the community and its tuition centres.

The Eelam community has helped a total of two-and-a-half lakh people affected by the floods in TN and continues to help them. 'Refugees are not hapless people. Give them a chance to help themselves,' Poongkothai said. 'Our refugee community now has doctors like young Sruthika and many engineers. Of course, it's not easy for them. They don't get jobs in India. Still, the fact that they are empowered means something. Tomorrow, they can even go back to Sri Lanka and work in their own hometowns.'

Refugees helping the host nation also changes the equation a bit. It offers them a sense of power, which the tag of 'refugee' robs from them. 'Before, they were refugees. But now, they are welcomed when they go to Indian schools. They are treated with a lot of respect because these are now people who help school children with shoes, and volunteer for capacity building. They are beyond local politics. In the villages, there are all these power struggles, but when they tell them, "We are Tamil refugees," there's no politicking. Nobody interferes. People also listen to them. When rich people or you and I go and counsel people or tell them, "Don't worry, you'll be okay," those affected by disasters will ask us, 'What do you know? You go back to your air-conditioned room," and rightfully so. But when our refugees, who live in worse conditions sometimes, tell them, "It will be fine," there is a sense of camaraderie. Those affected say, "If you survived, I could too perhaps." The biggest thing that's come out of this for our refugees is this sense of dignity and pride, which is very important for all of us.'

Memories of Cooum I

Back in the seventeenth century, the man in control of the eastern coast (the 60-km stretch from Pulicat to San Thome) was Damarla Venkatapathy Nayak. His brother, Ayyapa Nayak, offered East India Company's Francis Day—whom the late chronicler of Madras, S. Muthiah, calls 'a hard drinking, enthusiastic gambler and lusty womaniser'[85]—a strip of land for a rent of 600 pounds, to build a factory. Day chose that spot, which had all but sand and was struck constantly by cyclones and tidal waves, a little away from the friendly Portuguese–Indians at the St Toma (today's Santhome, Mylapore), because the factory needed 'good anchorage for ships', 'natural protection from thieving hordes of horsemen' and the 'proximity of good markets for exchanging commodities'.[86]

The city of Madras, writes Henry Davison Love in 1913,[87] owes its name to the headman of the fishing village on the banks of the Cooum River. Day's factory was to be set up on the thope, or grove, of a Catholic named Madarasen, with the promise that it would be called Madarasenpatnam.

Although, the Nayak brothers wanted the settlement to be named after their father Chennappa Nayak as Chennapatnam.

Thus was born Madras that is Chennai.

Rao Bahadur R. Krishna Rao Bhonsle says in an essay on the origin of the word Madras,[88] that Madarasen must have taken that name when he converted to Christianity in remembrance of his benefactors, the Madra family. This became apparent when the tombstone of Manuel Madra was discovered in July 1927 at the St Lazarus Church of present-day Mylapore. The Madra family was known for rebuilding a church—which used to exist back in 1582—in 1637.

There is, of course, no historical record of the genealogy of the city's name. It could have also come from Makhras Kuppam, named after the Marakkayars, who come from the lineage of Muhammed Ali Walajah, nawab of Arcot.

If the Company's business had reached, could colonial takeover have been far behind? It was from this piece of land that lay between the Cooum on the south and the Elambore River in the north—which would become part of the Buckingham Canal—that the foundations of India's first city were laid on 22 August 1639. Around this factory and the Cooum, Madras was born.

Yet, there is too little glory for the Cooum in our history.

Say the name Cooum to someone from Chennai and watch them find many creative ways to use it, except to refer to a water body that gushes forth with mirth to the sea. The name now can only mean one thing to this city and its people—an assault on its olfactory senses. Cooum is what you say someone's mouth is like when they speak filth. Cooum is what your street smells like when sewage overflows. Cooum is what your home looks like when it's dirty. Cooum is much like the word uncouth. You can smell it in the back of your head, even before you mouth it. No buses were ever burnt for the Cooum, nor were protests held with rail and road rokos, not here. No demands for management boards, no farmer awaits her arrival. No one buries themselves in sand for her. No IPL matches boycotted, black flags shown to prime ministers, and no film releases stalled. No one marches for her or her sisters from this city. Not when she flows with sewage, not when she fills up people's homes with sludge and human excreta, and not even when we finally see her full, once a decade, during the heavy monsoon, and hope for her to stay that way, only to be disappointed again because of all the filth she is forced to carry on her back later.

Chennai-based writer–historian Venkatesh Ramakrishnan has worked on culturally mapping the Cooum over the years. He has written extensively about significant battles fought and won by glorious Tamil kings of yore, on the Cooum's banks, which then laid the foundation for the spread of Tamil culture to lands far beyond our shores, and how cinema and architecture that today have come to define the city, as well as its tourism and heritage, flourished on the banks of this river. The Cooum, historical accounts show us, was once shelter to crocodiles and four dozen varieties of fish, and back then it was called the Thames of South India.

The river originates from the village Cooum in Thiruvallur district, and is not dirty all the way. Between its hometown and the Paruthipattu Anaicut, a check dam across the Cooum in Chennai's Avadi area, it flows in all its pristine glory, taking care of the town's water needs. According to Priya Baskaran, author of *The Gods of Holy Koovam*, there is even a *Koova Puranam*, which is part of a larger spiritual text called *Skanda Puranam*, in which the Cooum is said to have originated from the bow of Lord Shiva.[89]

The Cooum's glory seems to have waned as Madras grew around it. The last time it was clean enough for a royal bath was in the early nineteenth century. The palace of Umdatul-Umara, the nawab of Carnatic—extending from the Cooum on the one side to the beach on the other—was almost always enveloped by the beautiful strains of the veena, and in particular the sarang raag that the nawab so loved, during his reign of the Carnatic state between 1795 and 1801. If the ladies of the palace were not listening to music or visiting the beach, now the sprawling Marina, to enjoy a moonlit night or the rising of the sun, they were out bathing in the Cooum.[90]

Madras's grievances against the Cooum are not new though. While it is true that this river, called the bountiful canal of Walajah in 1790, has been ruined by years of neglect, here's a stinker of a fact: there is reason to believe that even before the city of Madras was founded, some parts of the Cooum were always smelly.

Frank Penny, speaking of why the fort was set up where it was, wrote even in 1900:[91]

> It was nothing but a dreary waste of sand, on which a monotonous sea broke in a double line of surf, giving it an inhospitable look, which it retains to the present day. A shallow lagoon-like river, running parallel with the sea for a short distance, formed the protection needed on the land side from predatory tribes of horsemen; but otherwise the river was useless. It afforded no shelter for ships; and its brackish waters were of no use for irrigation purposes. It often emitted an unpleasant and unhealthy effluvia from the rotting seaweed lying in its loathsome black ooze. The river, confined to narrower limits in the present day, with some of its mud

> banks reclaimed, is scoffingly dubbed "The Silvery Cooum". To atone for its defects, it has a trick of assuming in the tropical sunset a fascinating beauty and fairness. Its smooth waters reflect the gorgeous colours of the sky; the blue smoke of the wood fires in the native huts spreads an aetherial azure haze over the palms and banyan trees on its banks, and the eye of the artist is equally delighted as his nostril is offended when he gazes across its broad bosom. When the sky is purple with the gathering clouds of the monsoon, the Cooum ruffles its waters into a sheet of silvery grey ripples, and it gleams in its setting of dark green like a polished mirror of steel; even the black wet ooze glistens with delicate shades of pearl. But the Cooum is not remembered for its false and transient beauty; it is indelibly stamped on the memory of the Anglo-Indian by its odours.
>
> Neither the smell of the river nor the acres of sandy waste discoursed the persevering servant of the East India Company, and Day concluded his negotiations satisfactorily on the 1st of March, 1639–40. And by his transaction his employers obtained their first territorial rights in India.

Much of what Penny wrote about the Cooum holds true even today. And even as the British were thriving in and around Madras, Florence Nightingale, who was alarmed at Madras's water and drainage conditions, sounds as upset as any of us today about the Cooum when she wrote:[92]

> At Madras the "sanitary state" is called "good" and the commander-in-chief himself adds, if the vile stinking river Kooum were not under the very noses of the 'patients'. Both cholera and gangrene have appeared at times in the hospital. ... For some hospitals the "impurities" are removed by hand

> carriage to 30 yards from the hospital. In another, the privy is said to be a "disgrace to the 19th century". One wonders to what century it would be a credit.

Even in the twenty-first century, we have not been able to rid our state of manual scavenging. It is not uncommon in Chennai to catch sight of men who are forced, through an exploitative system, to go into underground manholes and unclog sewage holes with their bare hands, while in our villages, men and women are made to carry untreated 'impurity'. Tamil Nadu also has the highest number of manual scavenging–related deaths: 144 between 2013 and 2018.

In November 2016, I met three safai karamcharis, employed by a private contractor for the cleaning of a manhole in the posh RA Puram in Chennai. All three were then living in Jafferkhanpet, where ten families were scraping by with work delegated by contractors, who were, in contravention to law, sending the workers down manholes without proper gear for a pittance. All three had lost their homes in the floods of 2015 and as a result, were living on the terrace of an apartment building, and even after a year, had not been rehabilitated. One of their relatives was admitted in the general hospital after catching an infection inside a septic tank. The doctors said he might lose his arm. And then struck demonetisation in November 2016, which would snatch away even their regular work, as contractors operate entirely in cash.

Chennai owes Nightingale a great deal for her writings about its state of sanitation. The city, in fact, owes its drains to her recommendations.[93] 'But the capital of Madras Presidency is perhaps most astounding. Its river Koovum is a Styx of most offensive effluvia. The air in Black Town and Triplicane is 'loaded with mephitic effluvia at night'. The atmosphere around Perambore and Vepery is 'perfectly poisoned', she wrote. In her letter to *The Illustrated London News*, she again called the Cooum, 'till lately of most unsavoury and unhealthy reputation.'[94]

In this report about the state of sanitation in the three presidency towns, she said, 'Bombay, it is true, has better water supply; but it has no drainage. Calcutta is being drained; but it has no water supply. ... Madras has neither.'[95]

An Unequal Flood

Everyone in the city remembers the day the floodwater drained out, differently. Some were relieved, some were still in shock, some continued to look for loved ones, while others came home to devastation. But for almost all of us it was heartbreak. The city wore its defeat for days and nights on end. For a week after the floods, on the footpaths outside most homes were stinking piles of mattresses, pillows, quilts, cushions, straw mats, bedsheets and swollen rotting wood and food grains, and cars left open, even as the sun came down hard on us, making a mockery of it all.

Entire homes were being emptied out, like in my parents' case. And before you knew it, the city was on the verge of a crisis. A garbage crisis. Thousands of sanitation workers from across the state were called in to Chennai by the government. And these workers had to deal with a city that had dragged decades of filth from its river beds, lakes and all kinds of things from people's homes on to the streets, as well as animals that were handed the death sentence—about 100,000 tonnes of putrid trash.[96] Apart from extricating dead human bodies from nooks and crannies, which had washed away in the flood, sanitation workers also had to deal with people defecating in the open, as flood-hit public toilets were non-functional.

The city's sanitation workers, many of whom had their own homes destroyed, also reported back to work because they needed the money. They live outside the city, because of slum relocation drives, and neither help nor warnings had reached any of them. The city of Chennai clearly felt no senjotrukkadan for its brethren who came from other cities to clean it, it would appear, and instead ill-treated them.

Hundreds of workers complained that they were transported to and from their work places for the day in the same lorries in which they had transported garbage all day, exposing them, without proper protection gear and aid, to trash and diseases, and that they were treated worse than 'kothadimaigal'—bonded labourers. Several workers—who were involved in other trades before being engaged by the municipality for cleaning (agricultural labourers, electricians, and quarry workers)—complained of cuts, bruises and illness from the prolonged exposure to garbage as well as bleaching powder.

Many newspaper and independent media reports during the floods spoke of the poor conditions under which sanitation workers were being made to work. They also pointed out that help had not reached north Madras or the working class populace affected by the floods in the southern parts outside the city limits.

~

In a scathing report on the relief work related to the November floods that affected Cuddalore district, titled 'Tsunami to 2015 Floods—No Respite For Dalits In Disaster Response, Tamil Nadu', the National Dalit Watch–National Campaign on Dalit Human Rights, and Social Awareness Society for Youth Tamil

Nadu said that 'in most of the places Dalit households have complained about the wilful negligence of government and other agencies of assessing the losses occurred to Dalits.'[97]

Many of the workers who were exploited by the state and made to work in dangerous conditions in the aftermath of the floods were temporary employees. Writing in detail for the *Hindustan Times* on the issues faced by the sanitation workers, Sudipto Mondal reported on 11 December 2015, 'As many as 78 men from the Dindigul municipality are camping in a marriage hall in Gajalakshmi colony of Chennai. They were provided with only seven gumboots. None of them have been given gloves, masks, soap or oil. These luxuries haven't been granted to local sanitary workers either. ... Here is another well-known fact: all of Chennai's and indeed all of Tamil Nadu's sanitation workers are either Dalits or Adivasis. Most of them are from the Arunthathiyar Scheduled Caste. ... Only around 700 of the 7,000 sanitary workers in the city are permanent employees of the corporation and get above ₹15,000 per month. The rest are on contract and are paid anywhere between ₹200 and ₹290 as daily wages. No work means no pay. There are no sick leaves.'

Forty-two-year-old Palanichamy, who was brought to Chennai from Sholangapalayam in Erode, and Kantha Rao from Chennai, died as they were made to work under unsafe conditions for prolonged hours, while on duty, cleaning up the city. Conservancy workers had to clock over twenty hours cleaning up the garbage piled up everywhere. Adhiyamaan, founder of the Aathi Tamizhar Peravai—the Arunthathiyar movement that aims to 're-establish Arunthathiyar's economic, cultural and social status'—also rued the fact that sanitation workers were not treated with even basic human dignity and that 400 of them had to share two toilets. They were not given glasses to drink water from and had to drink water using their plates. He also said that many workers were paid a paltry sum of ₹50 per day for their work.

He asked, 'Is this the right way to treat government employees? If a government servant who's working as a peon, for instance, was being asked to travel, he would be given an advance or a TA/DA [travel and dearness allowance], right? They were given nothing of that sort and, to add insult to injury, transported in inhuman ways—in lorries, as if they were cows and goats—from far-flung districts like Ooty and Gudalur. Someone came from out of town to clean Chennai and died because of this. How did they decide that these people didn't deserve the same kind of transport, stay and treatment that is offered to government employees who travel on work? In any case, what was the need to bring people from other districts to clean the city? Why didn't they use machines to clear the debris everywhere, which would have been faster anyway? Many of them weren't given any safety gear, neither gloves nor boots. People who belong to only one particular caste are doing this work. Our casteist society and people belonging to other castes think that these people were born only to serve others as if they are slaves. A deeply entrenched casteism among everyone here is the reason that these workers were treated this way.'

He also pointed out that people say, 'This is their job, their duty. Let them do it.' He added, 'It is because of this mentality that even now, every month people die of toxic gas from sewage holes in our state. These are people who have been forced violently to perform these jobs because of the caste system. Nobody who's doing this work enjoys it.'

To those who ask, 'Why are you doing this job? Find something else,' he said, 'Even today in our villages, people are punished if they do not do this work that is heaped on them by other castes. Our belief is that not just our people, no human being should be asked to engage in manual scavenging and sewage cleaning. Use technology and machinery entirely. Everyone, including politicians, maintain silence when it comes to this topic alone. Why is there no political and societal will to end manual scavenging in our country, despite the laws?'

He also said that this lack of will 'shows the absence of humanity in this country.' And that only when mankind finally becomes humane, this problem will be solved. 'Until then, we will have no solution.'

Comrade Paramasivam, state vice president of Louis Sanitation Workers Union (affiliated to New Trade Union Initiative) had said in an interview to Thozhilalar Koodam, a blog that presents 'news coverage, analysis, legal information, personal stories, and art that engages with contemporary labour issues in and of interest to Tamil Nadu,' that more than 150 workers 'were brought from the districts of Nellai, Tuticorin and Kanyakumari. Earlier, they were housed in a marriage hall in Thiruvottiyur which was adequate for the workers. After three days, they have been shifted to Kodambakkam where already more than 500 workers are being housed. The lack of water and toilets has forced these workers to shell out as much as ₹25 per day to wash themselves. Workers were falling sick and were seeking treatment by themselves. While the government has provided anti tetanus injection, no comprehensive health infrastructure is available for the workers and the workers need to fend for themselves. ... While food is being taken care of by the government, the workers had to arrange their own transport and spending for civic amenities is creating hardship. The workers had brought their own materials from their hometown and had to use them.'[98]

Rajashekar, who was brought from Salem for sanitation work, said, 'There weren't even toilet facilities for us. We were in Chennai for a week staying in a wedding hall, all of us sleeping on the floor. They didn't even give us proper food. We were given kanji and koozh. Not even a proper meal with rice, and were made to work for hours on end.' Senthil Kumar from Namakkal said, 'We were told that we would be able to go back home in four days. Even after a week there was no sign of them sending us back home. I had ulcers in my throat from spraying bleaching powder all day long. I was unwell and wanted to go home and there was no sign of us being sent back.'

People were so angry over the lack of help in North Chennai that according to Sruthisagar Yamunan, who wrote in *The Hindu*,[99] 'There were flash protests across the region against non-availability of essential items in the past two days. ... Residents blocked the Vallalar Nagar Bridge and shouted slogans such as, for the government, Chennai starts and ends at Poes Garden and Gopalapuram [where the then opposition leader Karunanidhi lived]. They said, "We have never been considered residents of Chennai and today you can see the effects of this."'

Neglect compounded when it came to further marginalised groups. Trans people were invisibilised in these floods by nearly everyone even as they suffered discrimination that was manifold. Several trans women in and around the Tiruvottiyur area in North Chennai, as well as those who lived in Saidapet near the Adyar and along the Cooum river, alleged complete neglect from authorities. Only spaces that worked for sexual minorities in the city such as Sahodaran, Orinam, Snehidhi, Thozhi and Nirangal helped the community.'[100]

The discrimination was further exacerbated in villages such as Marakkanam and Cuddalore along the coast, which were also affected by the floods, and the locals complained that people from dominant castes cornered the relief material. Writing for the *Economic and Political Weekly*, J Balasubramaniam of the Intellectual Circle for Dalit Actions said,[101] 'During the fact-finding conducted in 18 villages it was found that hundreds of houses belonging to Dalits were damaged partially or completely. Thousands of daily wage labourers have lost their means of livelihood and in almost all the villages the danger of an epidemic was imminent and people, especially children, women and elderly people were suffering from health disorders. ... Though the flood equally affected both Dalits and non-Dalits, we could not find a single relief camp where both Dalits and non-Dalits were given shelter and this amounts to the tangibility of discrimination in practice. In most of the villages the relief material was brought to Dalit villages after getting caught in local power relations, where both the dominant castes and locally powerful politicians prevented and delayed the distribution of relief material. Villages where there is large-scale discrimination in practice like, Kaaduvetti, Varagurpettai and Onankuppam, the relief materials brought by the NGOs for distributing among the Dalits was prevented by the dominant castes. Moreover, the unaffected dominant caste villagers pillaged all the materials.'

This fact-finding committee was made up of 'Anbuselvam, an independent researcher based in Puducherry, Stalin Rajangam, a writer based in Madurai, A. Jeganathan, a researcher based in Madurai and J. Balasubramaniam, an academic based in Madurai'.

Denial of access to relief and rehabilitation based on caste, amounts to hate, and is against the safeguards the Constitution offers India's Dalits. The country's disaster management plan and, in particular, Tamil Nadu's, needs to heed the voices from within the Dalit community. The government must take discrimination into account and come up with ways to tackle the same during disasters. The International Dalit Solidary Network in September 2013 offered several recommendations in this regard including asking the state to: recognise that caste-based discrimination happens during aid distribution, perform social equity audits, use participatory methods, design specific approaches for complaint redressal, understand pre-existing vulnerabilities of Dalits and other excluded groups, as well come up with legislation and policies to tackle all these.[102] Asia Dalit Rights Forum, in a report titled 'Sustainable and Resilient Communities: A Profile of Dalits in Disaster Risk Reduction in South Asia', said,[103] 'It is incontestable that disasters hit the vulnerable sections of the society such as women, persons with disabilities, and groups that are socially excluded and discriminated based on their identity emanating from caste, religion or ethnicity. ... The socially excluded communities, especially the Scheduled Castes and the Scheduled Tribes, disproportionately bear the consequences of climate change. Already residing in the least hospitable environment in urban and rural areas, including forests, they are the first and most severely affected. They are the last to get relief and sometimes are actively prevented from getting relief. Yet, the present institutional mechanisms for disaster management do not recognise caste induced vulnerabilities. Casualties and damage or loss of properties, infrastructure, environment, essential services or means of livelihood on such a scale are beyond the normal capacity of the affected Dalit communities to cope with. There is a need for proper state support to develop the adaptation mechanism of Dalits and support livelihood diversification strategies.'

Families of Chennai's own sanitation workers living in far flung areas of the city in poor neighbourhoods were left to their devices for long after the floods. In Semmenchery, 400 contractual public sanitation workers—those who work as domestic help, auto drivers, daily wagers in construction sites and security or service staff in the IT corridor—were on their own. Sujata Mody, president of Penn Thozhilalar Sangam and national secretary of the New Trade Union Initiative, writing for *Scroll.in* said,[104] 'Some of the sanitation workers live in the slum clearance board colony of Semmenchery, to the south of the city. At 5 a.m. on Tuesday, they were warned that the nearby Perumbakkam Lake would breach its banks and they had an hour to get to safe ground. This was an improvement on a fortnight ago, when the lake overflowed without warning at 3 a.m., flooding their homes, sweeping out their belongings and closing off the exits of the colony's inner streets. At the time, the nearly 5,000 families were left stranded without electricity, water or food.'

The poor and the disadvantaged of Chennai who would have needed the most help to come out of this disaster, have all had to rebuild their lives, with practically no help from the state.

Memories of Cooum II

The Cooum has for long suffered abuse, and its fate seems to have been sealed at the hands of the Nayak who gave away the land to the imperial force, and later, our own politicians would inherit this river and find themselves confounded by its needs. In 1937, at the Madras Legislative Assembly, Basheer Ahmed Sayeed, who went on to become a judge, in his speech at the assembly said,[105] 'Then, there is the river Cooum, that ancient river Cooum that flows through the city,' and asked for two minutes to talk about it. 'The Cooum is owned by the Government. They make an income of Rs 40,000 or Rs 50,000 therefrom, but they spend not a single pie for its improvement,' he lamented.

A year before Independence, the Cooum made an appearance in the assembly again, and the man who was once the mayor of Madras, Abdul Hameed Khan, rued the conditions of the Buckingham Canal and the Cooum and suggested ways to improve them. The records of the assembly's debates for 1946[106] contain words that ring true even today. 'Then we have got the famous Cooum. This is an eye-sore and a thing which will be a disgrace to any civilised government or to any city. It has been allowed to lie like this for ages, and the view that the Government of Madras has been taking that it is the duty of the Madras Corporation to attend to it is wrong'.

There was even talk about taking the help of experts to divert the course of the Cooum that year. And then, fast forward to 1966, they are still talking about it, this time at the Madras Legislative Council (which was later disbanded in 1986). 'Sir they should prevent the stink emanating from Cooum River. The University is on the banks of the Cooum. I should like to repeat that we are not living in a "city beautiful" but we are living in a "city dreadful". We are talking of slum improvement all the time. But I wish to mention this to the Hon. Minister for Health and the Minister for Housing that many parts of Madras City are stinking because of sullage being led into the Buckingham Canal,' a member of the house rued on 5 November 1966.[107]

It was the 'dream' of the erstwhile TN chief minister, Annadurai, to clean the Cooum, and he inaugurated a clean-up scheme in 1967 with the promise that it would soon sparkle like the Thames of London. He also said that his PWD minister, Karunanidhi, had insisted on financial allocation for the same. Indeed, it had also been a lifelong dream and promise of Karunanidhi, one of Annadurai's political heirs, to clean up the Cooum. Karunanidhi even briefly set up a regulator and a sand pump at the river's mouth—near Napier Bridge, where the sand bars were the chief cause for the Cooum's contents being blocked from entering the sea—and built a walkway, 'removed encroachments', diverted sewage, and later even inaugurated a pleasure boat service in 1973 as the chief minister of the state.

Alas, it would all be short-lived and it would not be long before the pumps stopped working. M.K. Stalin, who was the deputy chief minister in 2010, inherited not just the party from his father Karunanidhi but also a Cooum clean-up dream. Stalin had spoken of turning the Cooum beautiful in less time than it took Singapore to clean its river—a decade. Singapore too, while cleaning its river and turning into a bustling economic powerhouse, had evicted countless hawkers, fishermen with their bumboats, farmers with small farms, and all those living in shanties around the river and moved them into high-rise buildings.

It was also under Stalin's mayorship that the catchphrase Singara Chennai, or Beautiful Chennai, was coined. ₹3,000 crore have gone down this Cooum drain, literally, as this clean-up and beautification project has been started, stopped, re-started, stumbled, bruised and battered over the years. Subsequent governments have inaugurated schemes repeatedly, as the Cooum continues to stink to the high heavens to this day. Stalin's Singara Chennai dreams remain elusive, and there is now a common joke that it is actually Sinkara Chennai,[108] a Chennai that sinks. To his credit, however, it was under Stalin's watch that the beautiful Adyar poonga, which involved the restoration of degenerated wetlands—the Adyar's estuary and creek—was set up by the Chennai River Restoration Trust. The project was conceived by the Jayalalithaa-led AIADMK government in 2006 and was inaugurated by the DMK-government led by Karunanidhi in 2011.

Successive governments have also inherited similar ambitions for cleaning up the city and its rivers. In a country like India, and in a state like Tamil Nadu, who decides what is clean—be it Singara Chennai or Swacch Bharat? In Pa. Ranjith's hugely popular film, *Kaala,* which addresses the displacement of the poor and even makes a direct reference to Singaara Chennai towards the end, the protagonist asks an interesting question about these dreams. Where do we draw the line between purifying the city and purging the poor out? In the name of resettlement and redevelopment, do we want to move them from their own homes, from horizontal slums to vertical slums far away from the development they ushered in with their labour? There is no doubt that the working class comes entirely from these slums in Chennai, and that there is not just a class divide but also one involving caste. Also, it is not as if one fine day people decided to just come and camp out in these river banks. There is a historic reason for the banks of the Cooum playing host to certain communities. C.S. Srinivasachari writes:[109]

> In 1734, the Governor (Morton Pitt) received proposals for building a weavers town immediately adjacent to Black Town. Sunka Rama, who was dismissed from his post of Chief Merchant in 1731 and had fallen out of favour, had an extensive garden in the loop of land almost encircled by the Cooum, where it takes a bend before flowing into the sea. This garden measured 804 yards by 500 yards, contained many trees of substantial growth and enjoyed a good supply of water. The Governor alleged that the cowle of Sunka Rama giving him right of possession for this garden, was not in proper form and defective, because it had been made without the consent of the Council and without the receipt of any consideration. Sunka Rama protested, but to no purpose. The garden which was flanked by the Cooum on one side and Periamet on the other, was resumed by the Government which resolved to settle therein several hundred families of spinners, weavers, painters, washers and dyers along with Brahmans and dancing women and other necessary attendants of the pagoda. The village was to be called Chintadre Pettah.

This area, today called Chintadripet, was originally Chinna Thari Pettah, the village of small looms. In *Madras Rediscovered,*

S. Muthaiah sums up the birth of this village with his pithy commentary thus, 'The commercialisation—slumming—of the Cooum had begun. It has been going on ever since.'[110]

A wonderful recreation of this historic event is seen in writer Tamil Prabha's 2018 novel *Pettai*. In the introduction to this novel set in Chintadripet, Prabha not only manages to capture the colourful scenes leading up to the setting up of this village but also the caste tensions that pushed the marginalised from the centre of the village to the Cooum's banks, thus denying them access to the main streets except for when they had to perform their 'duties'. In Chintadripet back then, Prabha says in his book, the people compared the water of the Cooum to the sweetness of tender coconut water.

Whose City Is It Anyway?

During the floods, the Cooum carried 98,000 cusecs of water, flooding—though minimally and not as badly as the Adyar—parts of Avadi, Maduravoyal, Koyambedu, Chetpet, etc., and several parts had already been battered by the pre-flood in November. Even though the flooding along the Cooum was less, Chennai's civic bodies, in the name of flood mitigation and river beautification, have been on an overdrive to remove the poorest of the poor and the most vulnerable living along the banks of the river, to resettlement ghettos that are not only far away from the city and where wages are hard to come by but also are located on wetlands themselves.

Of course, not everyone is unhappy. Some have willingly left these 'hellholes' in the hope of living somewhere better, even if it means commuting hours to reach their jobs. But there are still many whose futures have turned bleak overnight because of the move. On the other hand, larger projects and encroachments by the elite along the river have faced minimal repercussions, if any.

Middle- and upper-class Chennai's dream for this river, include walking tracks, leisure activities, viewing points, fishing, angling, etc. Why not? There's even a stretch of the Cooum now within the city that does not look like a sewer anymore, because of such efforts. Every great city must have a place of beauty and leisure. But to look at the homes of the poor alone as an eyesore, before comprehensively addressing the issues of sewage treatment and garbage disposal, which contribute the most to the pollution of the river, and relocating the poor to places with no access to jobs, schools or health facilities, smacks of hypocrisy. All this, even as the government lets real estate builders continue to build on low-lying areas that will flood at some point, for sure.

What Chennai needs is perhaps not giant parks and waterfronts but roads that spill on to piazzas à la the ones pioneered by ancient Romans that continue to dot big cities world over. Little squares, islands of respite in the middle of all the chaos. Perhaps a fountain here, some trees there and some statues. Squares are egalitarian. Make better use of small nooks and pinch commercial establishments and parking lots, instead of displacing the poor and the marginalised.

Aggrieved by the forced displacement of people from Chintadripet, writer Tamil Prabha told me, 'The government is displacing us, people who've lived in Chintadripettai for generations after generations, from our land. Aindu Kudisai [Five Huts] is an important landmark of Chintadripet. Dalits live in large numbers adjacent to the Cooum here. Many moons ago, only five families lived here. Over the years, that number has grown to a bounty. Locally, it's been called 'Anju Kuchcha'. All these places that I breathed in are being razed to the ground and when I see it, old memories are rekindled and I feel an avalanche of sadness. All those who stood with bravado saying, "Idu enga area [This is our area]!" are today sitting atop piles of broken bricks, and are a picture of nerves. They are shunting out people who work in the fish market, prawn shed, Ritchie Street, Central and Egmore Stations' Parcel Office, to Perumbakkam [twenty-eight kilometres away from their workplace, almost an hour's drive and a few hours by public transport]. Particularly those who work in the fish market and prawn shed have to wake up as early as midnight sometimes to reach their workplace in the wee hours of the morning.'

To those, particularly in the administration, who say this is in the best interests of the people, that they now get to live in better homes away from the Cooum, the locals ask, 'What about the safety of our little boys and girls?' They now have to leave home early and reach home very late and worry about their children who are vulnerable to abuse, as they navigate a new area without adult supervision. Also, earlier, the people of a locality knew everyone there and lived together, but now people from various neighbourhoods have been put together in the same housing board and these too could lead to a lot of tensions.

'There are a lot of issues here,' Prabha added. 'Basic facilities like schools, hospitals and even water haven't reached Perumbakkam, and yet the government is hell-bent on moving people there with a great sense of urgency. Chennai's Dalit population is dwindling and fading. By pushing Chennai's identity outside, whose city does the government want this to become? This is not just displacement of people. This is an act of destroying Madras's identity and Madras's biggest cultural force. It used to be a vasadiyana [comfortable] city. It is now becoming a city for vasadiyanavargal [the well-off].'

Who Drowned Chennai?

In March 2018, the leader of the opposition in Tamil Nadu, M.K. Stalin, asked the government on the floor of the assembly why it had not tabled the CAG's audit report on the 2015 Chennai floods. The deputy chief minister, O. Panneerselvam, replied that the government had sought legal opinion from the advocate general, on 13 February 2018, on tabling it.[111] The CAG's report was submitted to the TN government on 1 June 2017.

That is when those of us following the flood story first got an inkling that perhaps the CAG had said something controversial. I filed an RTI application with the central CAG asking for the contents of this report the following month. My query was transferred to the Office of the Accountant General, TN and Puducherry, for 'necessary action.' 'It is requested that the information available may be furnished to the applicant directly under intimation to this office ...' the response said.

However, the 'necessary action,' it appeared, was a rejection note, even though the central authority had asked the state accountant general's (AG) office to share the information.

The final response from the department was:

> ... it is informed that the Audit Report on the said subject has been submitted to the Government for placement before

> the Legislature. The Report is a confidential document till it is placed on the floor of the Tamil Nadu State Assembly. Premature disclosure of contents of the said report would cause a breach of privilege of the State Legislature and hence the information sought in your application cannot be provided (Section 8 (1) (c) of the Right to Information Act, 2005).

This reasoning did not stand legal scrutiny, as, under Article 151 (2) of the Constitution, only audit reports relating to the accounts of a state have to be placed before the legislature. No other report comes under the purview of legislative privilege. Besides, Panneerselvam had said on the floor of the assembly that this report was not an accounts-related one.

I had also asked in my RTI application for the correspondence between the CAG and the state, and the reasons for the state's objection to this report. The answer was: 'The correspondence between the Government of Tamil Nadu and this office regarding the Report is also confidential as the Report is yet to be placed before the Legislature. Therefore, the same cannot be provided.'

Legal experts told me that there was no provision in the law that protected the communication I had asked for from public scrutiny or accorded it a legislative privilege.

My application had also asked for the reason offered by the state government for not tabling the report in the assembly, for which the response was: '... Government of Tamil Nadu has not given any reason to this office for not tabling this Report.'

I appealed further to the state AG for this set of information, because in addition to other discrepancies that showed the responses as less than satisfactory, under Section 8 (2) of the Right to Information Act 2005, '... a public authority may allow access to information, if public interest disclosure outweighs the harm to the protected interests.'

As the singular official document that sought to audit and place accountability for the floods, this report was significant. It should have been shown to the public as soon as possible, so that all the stakeholders, especially those of us affected by the floods, could learn the truth and take steps to avoid another disaster.

Moreover, the city of Chennai had the right to know why it flooded and who caused this flood, and this interest far outweighed any 'privilege' the people we elected to offices enjoy.

Lawyers and activists who regularly use the RTI told me how information never comes out from the government departments in the first instance. Unless one persisted through appeals, usually at least two rounds of it, what one sought would remain elusive.

Luckily for me, the same week a response to my appeal was due, the TN government finally tabled the CAG's report on the floods out of the blue, on the last day of the assembly session, 9 July 2018. This meant that no debate took place around the report. By the time this report came out, it lost its newsworthiness and was buried in the inside pages of newspapers.

Once this report was tabled, the AG office in Chennai readily dispatched responses to my other queries. Before I knew it, I was staring at 310 pages of responses—including correspondences as well as objections from various government department secretaries to the AG's office over the CAG report that had laid the blame for the flood squarely on the state government.

The 'Report of the Comptroller and Auditor General of India on Performance Audit of Flood Management and Response in Chennai and its Suburban Areas' minced no words while explaining just why this flood had happened: 'The agonising impact of the floods brought to public domain the failure in the roles, which ought to have been played by various Government bodies in effectively managing the disaster.'

In the 171-page report, the CAG explained the various reasons that may be attributed to these floods. The most scathing remarks in the report were reserved for the way the TN government had handled the tank that had caused the floods: On 1 December 2015, at 2 p.m., when the Chembarambakkam Reservoir had 3.377 TMC water—which was 0.268 TMC less than the total capacity of the tank—the amount being released from the tank was increased from 12,000 cusecs to 20,960 cusecs. Again, at 5 p.m., the discharge was increased to 25,000 cusecs and from 6 p.m. to 29,000 cusecs. The CAG felt that since the tank had space for another 0.268 TMC, the amount of water released from the reservoir could have been maintained at 12,000 cusecs for another six hours and even then the tank would not have reached the brim.

The auditors also came to the conclusion that this indiscriminate release of nearly 21,000 cusecs was made to save illegal encroachments in the foreshore area of the reservoir from submerging.

'This was a serious failure in operation of the reservoir, thus, contributing to the massive disaster. *Such imprudent and injudicious action by the Tank-in-charge as well as WRD warrants detailed enquiry* [emphasis added],' the report said. No action, however, has been taken based on these findings.

The report also pointed out that the indiscriminate discharge of water at 29,000 cusecs continuously for twenty-one hours from six in the evening of 1 December until three in the afternoon of 2 December into the Adyar River, in addition to the water from upstream tanks and catchment area, caused a huge flow of floodwaters into the river. It blamed the state's non-existent Emergency Action Plan—'due to GoTN's failure to update its system/manuals as per CWC (Central Water Commission) guidelines'—for the unsustainable manner in which water was released from the tank, drowning a hapless population, while also losing precious water that could have served the city during the dry months.

History seems to have repeated itself in Chennai. There is an uncanny similarity between what happened in 1877 in Adyar and what happened in 2015. Writing about the great wastage of irrigation water in 1877, William Digby said:[112]

> As an instance of the frightful waste of waters which occurred, the case of Adyar river may be taken. Nothing was done to conserve the water in its channel. For three days the river flowed full from bank to bank—250 yards wide at the Marmalong bridge. In the middle of the stream, for the width of one hundred yards at the least, the current was moving at the rate of two miles an hour: the depth of water was four feet on an average. It may be that there was not tank accommodation available for the storage of more water. But, even from the tanks, the waste was enormous. The Marmalong tank at Saidapett (a suburb of Madras) may be taken as an indication of the waste permitted. This tank, when it was seen by the present writer a few day's after the rain, was discharging over its waste weir a volume of water six yards wide and one yard deep, flowing at the rate of five miles per hour. The reason given for this outflow was that, if the water were retained, some of the banks of the tank might give way. Yet the level of the water in the tank was

> below what it frequently had been, and no disaster followed. The truth was this: the budget for petty repairs of tanks was so cut down at the beginning of the revenue year, that funds were not available for carrying out such precautionary works as were absolutely needful. The system by which works are done is so unsatisfactory that engineers, though they see the necessity for saving water, are unwilling to take the responsibility of keeping the water in the tanks, in the absence of that protection to the banks which they feel is necessary. They, therefore, choose the lesser of two evils, and, rather than risk a breach of the banks, with consequent flooding of the country around, and much damage, they consider it wise to let the water run to waste, and keep the level in the tank very low.

A good portion of the CAG's observations also pertain to planning or the lack of it in the state capital—no frequency-based flood inundation maps, no Emergency Action Plan for dams, no basin-wise comprehensive master plans prepared to respond to challenges posed by heavy rains, no law on Flood Plain Zone resulting in large buildings coming up on the banks of rivers and obstructing the free flow of floodwater, and no updated Water Policy. The report blamed the Chennai Metropolitan Development Authority (CMDA), which issues permissions for the construction of buildings and other development, for liberally allowing constructions in zones meant for other purposes, resulting in a steep increase in the built-up area. Such unauthorised constructions, it said, shrank the city's water bodies and led to massive inundation during the floods.

On encroachments, the report said, 'Despite enactment of a law in 2007 to protect tanks from encroachment, the percentage of tanks encroached, kept increasing year after year.'

The report also pointed out that eight drainage-related projects in Chennai that were part of the JNNURM were not finished because of encroachments and lack of coordination between different departments—a charge that would be made against the state's various departments over and over again in the years following the floods.

These incomplete projects, apart from poorly designed stormwater drainage networks, the CAG felt, contributed to flooding in many areas. This report also blamed the government for not taking desiltation work seriously enough and for not releasing funds for the same well before the monsoon. The CAG felt that the 'non-execution of works before monsoon hindered the free flow of floodwater' and added that this too led to flooding.

The report concluded that the Chennai floods of 2015 was 'a manmade catastrophe'[113] and found that the failures of various departments of the Tamil Nadu government had caused the floods. The word 'failed' appears thirty-eight times and 'failure(s)' forty-one times in this report.

Why This Report Was Buried

It is possible to guess why the TN government did not table this report for one whole year and sought legal advice before finally presenting it. Further communication that I accessed from the AG's office through RTI revealed that the chief secretary of the state, Girija Vaidyanathan, wrote a letter to the principal accountant general, TN and Puducherry, on 28 June 2017 about this report.

The state's senior officer felt that some of the observations in the final report—such as 'the Government wanted to protect an illegal patta land in the foreshore area from being submerged', 'indiscriminate discharge ... led to a man-made catastrophe', 'lack of seriousness attached to disaster preparedness on the part of the State Government' and 'reply was misleading and did not at all address the issue that the GoTN lacked an organised structure and approach for disaster preparedness'—'are sweeping in nature and do not have any evidential backing'.

She further wrote, 'It may be noted that if such unfounded observations find place in the final report, it would cause *serious embarrassment* [emphasis added] to both the state government and to the office of the Principal Accountant General.'

So, what exactly were the state's objections to this report? The AG's office revealed those too in response to my RTI query.

(I cannot emphasise enough just how important RTI is and why we must resist its dilution at any cost. The RTI gives us the right to peer beneath the iron veneer of bureaucracy and see just who is responsible for what. It is RTI that helped me find answers to questions about this flood that will stand legal scrutiny, and came to me written and signed by authorities, as irrefutable proof of the lax approach of the state and the measures it undertook in covering up its own shortcomings.)

In a 155-page response, various departments of the government such as the CMDA, PWD, Chennai Metropolitan Water Supply and Sewerage Board, Greater Chennai Corporation, and the office of the Commissioner of Revenue Administration sought to not only blame each other but also gave bafflingly silly reasons for the extremely serious charges levelled at them by the CAG. They were so incompetent in even defending themselves that, in fact, for two completely different allegations, the exact same answers were used word-for-word.

Just why is this 155-page report, with highly local, technical information, important? This report not only shows us the ways in which land belonging to all of us—our common properties, spaces that belong to us and to the state, spaces that are meant to act as buffer zones and help in mitigating floods—are written away slowly and steadily by people who do not possess the authority to do so, but also throws light on how the real estate industry as well as others, with the outright support of the state government's representatives and, in effect, the government, leech away mindlessly from what belongs to all of us.

The CMDA in its reply to the first draft of the CAG's report passed the buck to the local officials on several allegations—

for non-removal of encroachments, water channels covered in shrubs and bushes, and non-laying of even roads in Kundrathur, Perungalathur and Poonamalle areas.

While the entire reply docket seemed to be an exercise in obfuscation, which is possibly why the CAG did not take most of what was said by the state government into consideration and went ahead to file such a damning report, some of the most shocking revelations from this reply was the TN government's attitude to facts. While the CAG pointed out that the lack of communication equipment for rescue operations were a huge hindrance—a fact corroborated by news reports from that time, in which rescue personnel expressed the same concerns—the government, in its reply, said: 'communication was never a problem during the rescue, relief and restoration works'.

Responding to a question that asked why the government ordered excess sarees and dhotis and then distributed them as part of rations during Pongal, thereby misusing the Disaster Relief Fund, the Revenue Department said, 'Since the people affected by flood did not show interest, all the suppled [sic] quantity could not be distributed and they were utilized for the purpose of Pongal 2017, free saree and dhotis scheme.'

The CAG did not buy the government's explanation for releasing an extraordinary amount of water as being 'within the rules' and that the flood was caused by the rains. This, despite the state government giving pages and pages of garrulous explanation to recuse itself. The CAG's report stuck to its initial stand, despite refutations from the government, that the release of 29,000 cusecs of water in a bid to save illegal patta lands in the foreshore of the reservoir caused the 2015 floods.

The CMDA, in one reply, said, 'The contention of the Audit findings that the violation of the First Master Plan resulted in haphazard growth of the city, leading to adverse consequences such as congestion, impact on environment and flooding is not correct ....' This very first rebuttal from the authorities responsible for developments in the metro is troublesome.

In the rest of this response, the CMDA wilfully misrepresented what 'flood plain zones' mean. Their response to the allegation seeks to conflate the terms 'water body' with 'flood plain zones'. The CMDA claimed that the areas that are likely to be inundated are marked as water bodies in the city's master plan—'all the flood plain area which include river, pond, eri, and other low lying area which are classified as water body in the revenue records, have been zoned as water body in the Master Plan'. They also insisted that the maintenance of these areas vests with the PWD and the local body.

The CAG report mentioned several properties, complete with their plot number, that are in violation of norms and should not have been there. For many of these violations, the response of the development authorities was that the PWD gave these properties No Objection Certificates (NOCs). An NOC is required when a particular piece of development is near a coast, in the Coastal Regulation Zone (CRZ), as construction is not allowed up to 500 metres from the high tide line of the sea or 100 metres from the high tide line of the creek. The law says that 'the distance upto which development along rivers, creeks and back-waters is to be regulated shall be governed by the distance up to which the tidal effect of sea is experienced in rivers, creeks or back-waters.' The high tide line calculation in Tamil Nadu has in itself run into controversies.

Satellite imagery shows how the high tide line of the National Centre for Sustainable Coastal Management (which functions under the Ministry of Environment) ends much before a more 'robust line' proposed by the Institute of Remote Sensing, established by the Anna University, Chennai. The state government uses a manmade structure, a bridge at that, to decide where the tidal influence on the waters of the Adyar River end. It is the same bridge—the Maraimalai Adigalar or Saidapet Bridge—that was completely submerged, cutting off access to South Chennai during the floods.

In India, we have gone from taking the CAG's words too seriously to completely ignoring it. Some years ago, it was the CAG's report on the infamous 2G scam that was responsible for the misfortunes of the ruling United Progressive Alliance. The DMK and Congress parties lost the elections after these reports came out. However, the audit body's report on the flood had no repercussions for anyone.

Home on the River for Chennai's Elite

Among the many buildings that violate norms and are mentioned in the CAG report—like MIOT Hospital, which is built on the Ramapuram Nullah, a canal connected to the Adyar River—is an apartment complex abutting the Adyar. This complex is located right next to the Saidapet Bridge. And across the road, on the other side of this bridge, magically, the high tide line ends.

This swanky building is a mere few metres away from Saidapet's Thideer Nagar that has seen mass displacement of the marginalised in the aftermath of the floods. At ₹12,500 per square feet, a 2 BHK here will set you back by ₹1.76 crore, 3 BHK by 2.28 crore and 4 BHK by 3.50 crore. This apartment came up on the Adyar swiftly after the 2015 floods.

Building rules of the state stipulate that if 'a construction site is within 15 m of a water body, water course or well, such measure as may be necessary or as the executive authority may direct, should be carried out to protect the water body ….' This building is 9 metres away from the river. The CAG report has rightly pointed out that the CMDA continued to issue planning permission for buildings within 15 metres of water bodies 'without ensuring any ameliorating measures to prevent damage to the water body. CMDA adopted a procedure of obtaining No Objection Certificate (NOC) from WRD for issuing conditional approvals for constructions adjacent to water bodies. We observed that neither the TN Town and Country Planning Act nor the Development Regulations framed under SMP allowed CMDA to issue conditional approvals subject to adherence to NOC conditions of WRD.'

In its response to the allegation on the wrongful construction of this project on the Adyar, the CMDA said, 'During inspection it was noted that on the Northern side of the site, Adyar River is flowing. Therefore NOC from PWD was insisted.' The PWD issued an NOC on 12 May 2016, a second time after the 2015 floods.[114]

A division bench comprising Justices N. Kirubakaran and K. Ramasamy of the Madras High Court initiated suo moto proceedings against this building while hearing a petition on the eviction of families from the Adyar River's bank. The judges were sharp in their criticism of not only the construction but also the authorities who had given the nod for it in a flood-prone zone. They also sought answers from all the authorities responsible for the permissions that led to the building of this plot.

However, as it happens with most cases of this nature, especially suo moto proceedings, this one too changed course very soon. Portfolios of judges of the court changed and this matter was posted in front of a new bench comprising Chief Justice of Madras Vijaya K. Tahilramani and Justice M. Duraiswamy.

In January 2019, the counsel for the builders told the court that 135 families were suffering because of this case. He also said that the CMDA was not giving them the completion certificate or inspecting the site because of this case. The CMDA's lawyer also told the court that the project was constructed as per an approved plan.

The bench, in turn, asked the CMDA to carry out inspection and issue the completion certificate if everything was in order.

Everyone involved in this case, including those of us watching from the sidelines, know that the issue with this building is not whether it complies with the rules. It is about how rules were bent in the form of NOCs to make this building legal. The CAG report specifically pointed this out while saying that it is buildings like this that caused the flood. When the bench changed, the urgent questions asked by the previous bench were forgotten.

Presently, remedies for environmental transgressions in India are sought either through Public Interest Litigations (PILs) or through the National Green Tribunal, a quasi-judiciary body not staffed entirely by judges. It is indeed a matter of sheer luck, those working on environmental issues in this country will agree, that this matter originally came up before a bench of the high court that was able to see the whole picture, was interested enough in it and took it upon itself to summon everyone involved. Environmental activists should not have to simply wait around and hope that their matter will be posted before judges like this every time, in every court of the country. The other side, of course, of judicial activism is that in some cases there may even be an overreach. One of the judges who showed a keen interest in this case of encroachment, for instance, also ordered a blanket ban of the Tik Tok app across India while responding to a PIL in 2019, saying it spoils the futures of youngsters and mindset of children.[115] There are several cases, including some pertaining to these floods, which were in process, but reached a screeching halt when portfolios of the judges changed or judges were moved to the Supreme Court. The cases soon lost their relevance as well as sheen.

Epilogue

The Flood That Wasn't
—A Farce

* *The State's response in this farce is based on actual court proceedings*

The sounds of the beats grow heavy. Dama dama dama dama …

A man wearing a tandora and dressed in a white-as-snow dhoti, walks every street, under the gentle January sun, beating his drums.

'With this drum beat, it is announced, that a proceeding is now being initiated by the people of this city against those responsible for the floods of December 2015. All those interested may join the proceedings …' Dama dama dama dama.

On the call of the beats and the man's deep voice, a crowd collects. At first, there is only one woman following him, but soon she is joined by another and another, until every human in the city begins to follow the drummer, abandoning the haunted homes of the city, their vehicles, jobs, wounded pride, dead relatives and even gods.

They arrive at the beautiful Indo Saracenic style precincts of the Madras High Court. There isn't an inch of space left. It appears as if even ants cannot breathe here. But there is no chaos. There is anger. But this is no mob. If you looked at the crowd from above you would think this was a thiruvizha. But this is no celebration. If you pinched and zoomed out of the frame you would see nothing but a sea of humanity, round and round, in concentric circles. Knocking on the doors of justice.

It is morning and lawyers young and old are shuffling in and out of rooms, clad in black and white, the bands around their necks flapping up and down every now and then like curious cats. They are bewildered by this sudden influx of humanity, even as the skeletal CRPF staff struggles to let the crowd in.

'Which case are you here for?' a young jawan who was posted here after receiving a bullet to his leg at the border asks. 'Only petitioners are allowed into the high court.'

'Court vs Fort,' comes the answer from every single one of them. He has no choice but to let them in.

There are people everywhere on the campus. Near the Ambedkar statue that is adorned with fresh flowers, in front of the black statue of Sir Vanbakam Bhashyam, around the white statue of Thiruvarur Muthuswami, hanging by the intricately carved pillars and iron railings, the long, usually spacious corridors, the archways, and under the portraits of judges past ... At 10.30 a.m. sharp, the dawali strikes the gong near the court halls, seven times. Lawyers mill about, trying to get into their respective courtrooms. The crowd is respectful and gives them way.

Inside the Chief's court room, adorned in stained glass paintings, ornate antique furniture and long-stemmed ceiling fans, some of the petitioners wait, while others wait outside. A chopdar dressed in white, as his red and gold cummerbund glimmers, a silver staff in his hand, shushes everyone in the Chief's path, as lawyers give way and curtsy. The Chief is on his way to the courtroom. His hands are folded, he's saying namaste to the crowd, nodding and smiling. The crowd watches in amusement and murmurs to itself, 'That's the chief justice. He's here. He's here.'

The Chief, looking important in his black gown, enters the grand hall whose walls are covered in spectacular patterns, and the crowd rises. He sits in front of an ornate wooden panel, which too is decked with stained glass paintings. He is tall and genial. His moustache and hair have gained a respectable amount of greys over the years at the bar and the bench. Senior advocates are seated at a level lower than the judge, but higher than the crowd, upon an elevated platform, in beautiful old rosewood chairs. Bundles and bundles of important papers adorn every inch of the table in front of them as their juniors mill about with a sense of urgency, carrying copies of past judgements and consulting with members of the crowd, their clients.

'This court takes suo moto cognisance of the floods, and impleads Fort St George.'

A wild murmur of approval spreads through the corridors and spills on to the streets, where celebratory drum beats are heard. People break into dance, preliminary celebrations. They have no idea just how things work here. They think they are off to a great start.

Protestations, feeble, arise from the State.

'Once in 100 years. Rains ...'

People jeer.

'We must pin the responsibility somewhere. This will tell us where the blame lies,' the Chief says, and shrugs.

More feeble protestations, 'But ... but ... We are doing our best. Reservoir breach fear ...'

The Chief is in no mood to pay heed, as slowly, one by one, the senior advocates rise, representing various citizens asking to be impleaded. The Chief grants all of their wishes, as if he were a fairy godfather, with one swoosh of his hand. The crowds are elated again as joy spreads around like ripples in a placid lake.

Citizen A, a middle-aged man, with a French beard and wearing a Madras-checks shirt and grey trousers, submits to the court: 'The Compendium of Rules and Regulations [henceforth The Rules] on the basis of which the State purportedly acted during the Flood Events of Nov–Dec 2015 are in themselves hugely flawed, entirely archaic and not in consonance with the NDMA Guidelines on Management of Floods, 2008.'

'Hear. Hear. Yes. Indeed,' the angry crowd retorts, as women with babies in one arm, use the other to cup their chins in dismay, while men fold their dhotis in half and carry their older kids on their shoulders so they too can watch the proceedings.

'The same issues arise with the Chembarambakkam Reservoir as well,' Citizen B, a young woman wrapped in a red khadi saree, quips.

The Chief looks at The Rules and nods in disapproval.

Citizen A's lawyer, a senior advocate (SA1), now stands up. He wears his reading glasses and speaks slowly, yet deliberately and firmly. He elaborates on The Rules, his voice echoing through the corridors, and the crowd listens in rapt attention: 'Tamil Nadu does not have any reservoir exclusively designed for flood control though a few major reservoirs serve as flood moderators as well, among their multipurpose needs. Among the 42 reservoirs built on rivers so far, only four have a capacity above 1 TMC and below 5 and all rest are quite small with less than 1 TMC as their capacity. Their contribution to flood control is very limited. Besides there are a large number of small storages as irrigation tanks more densely spaced in the coastal districts to hold the north-east monsoon runoff which also contribute to flood moderation, though in a small way.' The lawyer then raises his voice, and removes his reading glasses. He waves it to further draw the judge's attention, especially to the next point, 'The unique feature in those tanks is that they are in chain one surplussing into another in its lower contour till all of them in the chain are full. While this helps in harnessing as much of the runoff as possible for use, there is the danger of all of them breaching and creating a bigger flood in the basin, if the first tank in the chain breaches. This leads to the added responsibility of maintaining standards of those small tanks to avoid breaching in normal course.'

The Chief writes something down, and the crowd is pleased. 'This is very important,' someone says.

SA1 finishes reading important excerpts from The Rules and adds, 'Milord, I want to bring to your attention to the date mentioned in Page 4 of Annexure 1.'

'Madras, 31st October 1984,' the Chief reads aloud while glaring at the State's representatives. 'These are the rules we still follow? They were made up in 1984?'

'The city and its limits have long developed and our rules are still from the 80s, Milord,' SA1 says.

Anger washes over all those watching this.

'How come land rates and taxes have changed and kept up but the rules you are meant to follow don't?' a voice from outside cries.

One would think the state's representative is pained, cornered, or at least sad and outwitted. That's where one would be wrong.

One does not understand how words work, and words, they work wonders in letting people off the hook. Words, they can be used to muddy the waters, make a mockery of righteous rage and pooh-pooh any claim.

Here's what standing up for the State, the old guard of the department-in-charge, an older man, with a long white beard, thunders, 'The Compendium of Rules for the Irrigation systems were meticulously framed by the experts in the field taking into account the rainfall, floods, etc., which occurred from 1904 onwards. The preface to the Compendium of Rules would amply prove the method of working out with the rules and for arriving at the design for the irrigation works.'

'What? What's he saying? What does it even mean?' people ask, expecting logic and reason in statements whose goals are obfuscation and meaningless banter meant to waste the time of the courts. People are silly.

The thundering from the man for the State continues, 'The petitioner cannot suo moto presume the rules as flawed without any technical basis. These rules have been found to be effective and efficacious for the past several decades.'

'Efficacious? What is he reading these days, Shashi Tharoor?' a woman in red saree rolls her eyes, as she fans herself sitting near the statue of Manu Needhi Chozhan.

'Merely because of the unprecedented flood in 2015, it cannot be said that the rules have become archaic,' the State lawyer says and sits down, as his peers pat him in adulation.

Now it dawns on the crowd. They see what is unfolding in front of them. As the words 'merely' and 'unprecedented' land upon them as if they are whiplashes. This is a *mere* flood for the people in power.

Recovering from this assault on their common sense in due time, the petitioners submit, 'The rules were issued on 31.10.1984 based on data from a Memo dated 18.07.1977. There isn't any reference, Milord, to any review or revision of these rules the last thirty-two years.'

The State's lawyer wishes to most respectfully laugh at the petitioner's demands.

'Change rules? Whatever for?' It's his turn to shrug as The Chief looks on helplessly. 'With all due respect, Milord, I don't know if you know this but the irrigation structures and other regulatory arrangements of Tamil Nadu are permanent in nature and cannot be altered. As are the designs of such structures. Revision or review and all, not at all required.' He now swishes his hands, as if he were the State's fairy godfather. 'Unless there is a change in the design of the irrigation systems ...'

'But what about the increase in population? Loss of flood plain? Loss of water bodies,' the eighteen-year-old engineering graduate wearing blue asks, as he gnashes his teeth, hugging a railing in despair.

'Has nothing changed since 1984 that required any review on the part of the government? What about desilting and technology to predict rains and floods?' the pluviophile in the crowd cries.

SA1 continues his thread of argument. 'I would like to illustrate just how archaic and outdated some of these rules are, Milord ... Chennai is consistently referred to as Madras throughout—even though the city's name was officially changed in 1996!'

'You mean to say, these people that fight with anyone who uses the city's old name and jump up and down to correct them are just using name changes as window dressing to hide their own inabilities? I am shocked,' a senior journalist murmurs to himself.

'These rules were framed and published in the year 1984 and there cannot be any deviation of the scope of rules due to *mere* change in the name of the city,' the State lawyer replies.

Things are now regressing to inanity.

'The rules talk about the use of a "cycle messenger" for urgent messages in case of rapid rise of water levels, your honour.' SA1 is losing patience.

'The flood controlling officer need not and does not stick to the rules for sending the messenger by cycle in carrying urgent messages,' the State says and the crowd is pleasantly surprised. A collective sigh is heard at last.

'Yeah, that's ridiculous, I am sure they just use a mobile phone now and do a WhatsApp broadcast or something,' a teenager quips.

But the State is not done dazzling everyone with its wit. Its lawyer continues, 'There is no bar for use of mechanised two-wheelers which is the current practice, Milord.' He beams with pride, and looks around at the crowd, utterly pleased with himself.

Eyes widen. A million palms rise to meet the respective million faces.

'Nothing. Better. Than. A. Mechanised. Two. Wheeler?' the sole trans woman lawyer in the crowd sits down, unable to process this incredulous piece of information.

SA1, growing agitated, stands up and throws his accusation out in the open, 'There is a clear failure in statutory duty to review and rewrite, Milord. Let me explain, the flood guidelines mandate the State Government/State Disaster Management Authority to complete a holistic review of reservoir rules so as to give flood control overriding priority by December 2009. Reservoir management, Milord, was highlighted in these flood guidelines as one of the three issues requiring special and immediate attention. These archaic rules are being used to justify the actions taken and not taken in December 2015 and, Milord,' he pleads, 'there is still no inclination to review or rewrite this!'

As if in a play, the bored State representative stands up, adjusts his thin rimless glasses, as his antique, expensive watch captures the sunlight and its reflection playfully bounces around the walls. He mechanically reads his excuse. It looks as if he has no idea what he is reading, though all the lawyers in the room know that it's only a ruse. Lawyers do things like this, saying vague unsatisfactory things when they have nothing to offer.

'The scope of the SDMA is comprehensive involving all the officials in the team of SDMA, while flood controlling is vested with the Flood Controlling Officer as per The Rules are localised pertaining to a particular water source. There was perfect and comprehensive reservoir management in Chembarambakkam Tank with close watch on the inflow during the incessant,' he hisses that word and continues, 'rains during November and December 2015 and as a result the structures of the Chembarambakkam did not suffer any damage. The storage was effectively managed and the flood discharge was also safely maintained to a maximum of only 29,000 cusecs, while the surplus discharge could be made upto 33,060 cusecs. The Full Tank Level, FTL if you will, was maintained at two feet below the maximum capacity during the concurrent period. The use of the term "archaic" by my learned friend is arbitrary, Milord.

There is no need,' he stresses, 'to review or revisit the same since there was no change in the design of the tank as the hydraulic features of the Chembarambakkam Tank are permanent in nature and cannot be altered. The petitioner has failed, Milord, to specifically mention any lacuna in the rules and has simply termed the same as archaic without any technical basis.' Adding insult to injury, the State hits the citizen below the belt with this: 'The *competence of the petitioner* to remark the rules as archaic is questionable. Rules cannot be rewritten on the basis of the recent floods. If necessary, necessary additions would be made.'

The stunned audience goes quiet. The silence rings through the hall and time seems to have stood still.

SA1, unlike the audience that is for the first time witnessing epic callousness coupled with absolute arrogance, is used to these techniques. He persists, nonetheless, 'Your honour, the data on which the Rules are based, is from 1977. What of the last forty years and the changes that have taken place? In particular, effects of natural and manmade silting, on both the reservoir and the Adyar River would not be taken into effect then? Rules appear to take a piecemeal approach for each reservoir/tank around the city with no reference to effect of events in the city and other tanks. This, in fact, Milord, has been specifically stated as a cause for flooding!'

At this point, the disgruntled State lawyer, with nothing to offer by way of explanation, begins descending to Tamil cinemasque courtroom rhymes and quips, 'The petitioner's professional competency to question the same is not holistic but pessimistic and his approach is only a vain attempt to find fault with the government on feeble grounds, which are technically invalid.'

It is the Chief's turn to cover his face with his palm and bury his shock with a mild clearing of his throat.

Like the valiant Vikramadittan who did not relent from his pursuits despite the Vedhalam's discouragement, SA1 persists, 'The Rules do not even provide any guidance as to what to do in the event of a breach of the reservoir. Milord, admittedly, a breach was only narrowly avoided that fateful night, 1 December 2015 when water reached 23.40 feet as against the FTL which is 24 feet. A disaster management plan for reservoirs was due by December 2010 and the State's approach is contrary to the spirit of the NDMA.'

Whereupon the State unleashes its biggest mockery upon its citizenry. 'The petitioner *imagines* that the breach was narrowly avoided on the night of 01.12.2015 even when the storage was not at FTL. The petitioner is once again proving his technical incompetence since any amount of flood can be effectively managed by proper regulation technique,' the State counsel says.

Citizen A launches into involuntary bouts of laughter at this sham even as Citizen B, who is yet to lose faith, says, 'But the flood was not prevented! They did not manage anything effectively. People died and homes drowned.'

The State counsel is steadfast in his disruptive role as the obfuscator par excellence and continues, 'The petitioner can refer to the book *Irrigation Manual* authored by Col W.M. Ellis published by the College of Engineering, Guindy and the 'Tamil Nadu Building Practices Code' pertaining to irrigation structures to deal with breach closing works in the irrigation systems. These are vague statement without any sound basis.'

The civil engineering graduate in the room cries a silent tear as he knows the year this manual was written in—1893.

SA1 reasons, 'The Rules vest officers with too much discretion, especially in the event of extreme weather events. These may have been appropriate given the technology available at the time of the framing of rules but with modern technology there is no need for such discretion. It allows for a large degree of human error, Milord.'

The State counsel at last displays an emotion. At the suggestion that power be taken away from his client, he deploys his original weapon—the thesaurus. 'The rule makers have in their wisdom framed the Rules such that the first flood controlling officer makes the decision regarding release of water by calculating the inflow and the possible discharge of surplus. The apprehensions of this individual are imaginary, hypothetical, non-specific and not based on any scientific basis.'

SA1 tries one last time to hit home, 'It is humbly submitted, Milord, that there is an urgent need to appoint an expert committee to review the Rules of the reservoirs at Chembarambakkam, Poondi, Red Hills and Cholavaram ...'

'No revision is needed your honour. Such an exercise would not help as these reservoirs are serving only the drinking water needs of Chennai and suburbs. The water cannot be depleted under *any* circumstances which would adversely affect the people with still higher risk of facing water scarcity. Even the Flood Patrol Rules did not allow the depletion of water while anticipating a flood. This petitioner is time and again putting forth the normal discharge effected from Chembarambakkam tank on 01.12.2015 and 02.12.2015, as if it deluged the entire city, without taking into account the enormous runoff realised in the own catchment of River Adyar between Chembarambakkam and Bay of Bengal. Every engineering personnel will agree that there was no flood discharge from Chembarambakkam Tank. The reservoir discharged only 29,000 cusecs while Adyar's carrying capacity is 72,000 cusecs,' the State counsel announced. Coolly. In effect, he is saying the Chembarambakkam had nothing to do with the floods while every newspaper and news article during the floods said it did. In fact, he was claiming that what had happened could not even be called a flood caused by the Chembarambakkam. You could call it that only if water had breached the reservoir, he says. Since the State had maintained water two feet below that level at all times, you would be wrong in calling it a flood caused by the reservoir.

'Then why did our homes fill up with water? Are you saying a flood never happened? Is this for real?' As the questions fill the courtroom, a sort of gloom descends on the faces of all present. They drop their drums, fold their arms and wait to see if the State would indeed deny the floods.

Citizen B's legal counsel, SA2, a woman in her sixties, wearing glasses with prominent thick black frames, stands up to point out the danger in the State's view that 'Flood Patrol Rules did not allow the depletion of water while anticipating a flood in the reservoir'. She argues that using water scarcity as an excuse, officials misused their discretions, and maintained dangerously high levels of water in the reservoir despite predictions for very heavy rains. 'It may be noted your honour that nowhere is it stated that the level should not be reduced in the event of an impending extreme weather.'

These too are dismissed as the ramblings of a non-technical personnel by the State.

SA2 waves a piece of paper at the counsel with logs from the Chembarambakkam Reservoir. She asks why no readings on the inflow and outflow at the reservoir were taken between 9 p.m. and 6 a.m. on 29.11.2015, 12 midnight on 31.11.2015 and 6 a.m. on 01.12.2015, and even on the day of the flood, during the critical period—10 a.m. to 4 p.m.—readings were taken only every two hours.

The counsel merely parrots his line about there being no flood at Chembarambakkam because the water had not breached the FTL and states as much bluntly.

'The stand of this respondent is that that there was no further rise of level due to increased inflow during the relevant time and instead, the flood controlling and other officers on site were constantly watching the bund and other regulatory arrangements.'

'Milord, the rules say that when discharge reaches 6,000 cusecs the first flood warning should go out and the second at 10,000 and third at 15,000. The discharge reached 6,000 cusecs between 9 and 10 a.m. on 01.12.2015 and exceeded it sometime between 6 and 9 a.m. and yet the first flood warning was issued at 11.20 a.m. only. That's a delay of 1 hour and 20 minutes. In fact, at 11.20 a.m. the discharge was more than 10,000 cusecs by which time the second warning should have gone out. The second warning went out at 1.32 p.m. with a delay of 3 hours and 30 minutes by which time the discharge was 20,000 cusecs. The discharge reached 15,000 cusecs sometime between 10 a.m. and 12 p.m. and there's no mention of a third flood warning having gone out anywhere.' SA2 and Citizen B are angry and this anger spills over to the streets.

'When we say the rules are old, they say they are full of wisdom and that it's all fine. But they haven't even followed their own rules. This is scandalous,' the old man in the front row, famous for many PILs and jail terms for pointing out lapses in the administration, shouts.

'The petitioner,' the State counsel says as the crowd settles down, 'is attempting to confuse with the rules which state that the flood controlling officer, that is the section officer, Chembarambakkam, should send messages pertaining to the discharge from the tank to the officers mentioned in the rules with the warning issued by the district collector of Chennai. Of course, there will be a lag between the two, they cannot be simultaneous.'

'Are you telling me that in 2015 it takes three hours for the district collector to receive a flood warning and issue it to the public?' The crowd outside begins to thin as the sun begins its descent. They quietly walk away, hitting their foreheads with their palms, for they realise what they are up against. 'Why do they call our bureaucracy the steel frame? They should call it a steel fort. It's impenetrable.'

'Milord,' SA2 continues to argue, 'They even began evacuating people only after the second flood warning, while the guidelines clearly say it should have been carried out as a precautionary measure based on warnings prior to impact.'

'Even then they evacuated only a fraction of the people whose homes were hit.' The people, whose houses had gone under, throw away the confetti in their hands, and leave in a huff from the high court. The building begins to look like its usual self.

Unfazed, the State counsel says, 'The district administration, local body and police have taken steps to evacuate the people living in low lying areas and abutting the river Adyar besides publicity through the visual and print media.'

'You cut off power supply remember? How will people watch these visual media?'

The women in the last row of the court hall leave.

'The respondent authorities are very much sure and confident that the floods in river Adyar were not due to the discharge of 29000 cusecs of water from the Chembarambakkam Tank but because of the runoff of the rainwater collected within the city limits and peripheries from the downstream of the Chembarambakkam Tank.'

'Why is this man talking as if nobody is responsible for the water bodies inside the city? Are they still not responsible for the overflowing of the Adyar?' The men in the front row begin to leave.

'Pch,' the counsel, emboldened by the emptying court hall, proceeds, 'the issue before this Hon'ble Court for adjudication is whether the water released from Chembarambakkam Tank alone was the root cause for the flooding in the Adyar. The petitioner is putting forth his personal opinion and own assertions which cannot be valid grounds for maintaining this writ.'

'This is clear obfuscation. Who is responsible for the water flowing in the Adyar through the city? Is it not the same authorities? I ... You ... What ... Nobody ...' Citizen A has had enough of this humiliating charade. He bows out.

Citizen B is unwilling to relent yet. It is simply the four of them now. Citizen B, her lawyer SA2, the Chief who has lost all hope and wants to simply head home, and the State counsel.

A despondent SA2 rises for the last time and says, 'I do not wish to waste this court's precious time any longer. Lordship, I simply have one last question for my learned friend. The Indian Meteorological Department's 'Summary and Forecast Bulletin', which is a publicly available document, has said on 21.11.2015 that there would be heavy to very heavy rain starting from

27.11.2015 and yet by the department's own admission it *swung into action* only by 30.11.2015. May we know why?'

'You see, Milord,' the counsel says with a drawl, as he too senses the end of the charade, 'Evidently, this advice was in generalised terms without indication about the heavy rain forecast in any particular locality.'

'Will the weather department start issuing forecasts for each and every street? What kind of excuse is this?' Citizen B leaves at last, defeated.

The Chief looks at SA1 and the State counsel, throwing his hands up in the air as if asking for divine intervention. 'I will consider and pass orders,' he says and goes home.

The day after, the Chief's prayers are answered, and as reward for his patience and penance, for sitting through hours of humbug, he is elevated to the Supreme Court.

Adjournments after adjournments have been awarded to the State following this, as the matter languishes in court with no end in sight.

Notes

1. R. Lenin, 'Kudimaramathu Scheme Fails Ryots,' *Deccan Chronicle*, 30 August 2018.
2. 'Adyar Swells Owing to Increased Discharge from Chembarambakkam', *The Hindu*, 4 November 2015.
3. Ibid.
4. Ibid.
5. Skymet Weather Services, skymetweather.com.
6. Vasanth Srinivasan, Srinivasan Ramani, 'A Wrong Call That Sank Chennai,' *The Hindu*, 10 December 20.
7. 'Damages Due to Heavy Rains Inevitable: Tamil Nadu Chief Minister Jayalalithaa,' Press Trust of India, 14 November 2015.
8. Nityanand Jayaram, 'Why is India's Chennai Flooded?' *BBC News*, 4 December 2015.
9. Vasanth Srinivasan, 'A Wrong Call That Sank Chennai, Srinivasan Ramani,' *The Hindu*, 10 December 2015.
10. 'Chennai in Crisis,' CSE Press Note, 3 December 2015.
11. 'Disaster in Chennai Caused by the Torrential Rains and Consequent Flooding,' Department-related Parliamentary Committee on Home Affairs, 12 August 2016.
12. Ibid., p. 7.
13. Ibid., pp. 11, 26.
14. Ibid., p. 11.
15. 'The Hundred Year Flood,' United States Geological Survey, usgs.gov/special-topic/water-science-school/science/100-year-flood?qt-science_center_objects=0#qt-science_center_objects.

16. 'Disaster in Chennai Caused by the Torrential Rains and Consequent Flooding,' Department-related Parliamentary Committee on Home Affairs, 12 August 2016, p. 13.
17. Order Dated 30 August 2016 in Rajiv Rai vs Government of Tamil Nadu, W.P. No. 39234 of 2015.
18. Order Dated 15 November 2016 in Rajiv Rai vs Government of Tamil Nadu, W.P. No. 39234 of 2015.
19. 'Schemes for Flood Control and Flood Forecasting for the Year 2017', Comptroller and Auditor General of India.
20. *The Private Dairy of Ananda Ranga Pillai (Volume II)*, Superintendent, Government Press, 1901.
21. *The Theosophic Messenger*, December 1909, p. 157
22. John Lane, *The Civilian's South India: Some Places and People in Madras*, The Bodley Head Limited, London,1921, p. 47.
23. In July 2014, when the Tamil Nadu Cricket Association Club denied entry to a dhoti-clad Justice D Hariparanthaman of the Madras High Court, the then chief minister, Jayalalithaa, called it an act of'sartorial despotism'.
24. Lane, *The Civilian's South India*, p. 47.
25. Ibid., p. 48.
26. Ibid., p. 200.
27. Ibid., p. 200.
28. Ibid., p. 201.
29. Allister Macmillan, *Seaports of India & Ceylon*, W H & L Collingridge, 1938, p. 284.
30. Humphrey Milford, *Madras Tercentenary Commemoration Volume*, Oxford University Press, 4 August 1939, p. 61.
31. A. Srivathsan, 'And Then Madras Was Bombed,' *The Hindu*, 5 October 2012.
32. Prince Frederick, 'Memories of Madras: Story of a Submerged City,' *The Hindu*, 22 November 2011.
33. Ibid.
34. Robert Bruce Foote, *Antiquities of South India*, 1916.
35. Kavita Kishore, 'Floods Turned Out to Be a Great Deal Harder for People with Disabilities,' *The Hindu*, 19 December 2015.

36. 'Popular Businessman V.G. Santhosam Evacuated His Luxurious House as Flood Water Enters,' *Thanthi TV*, 3 December 2015.
37. R.K. Radhakrishnan, 'Masterly Inactivity,' *Frontline*, 8 January 2016.
38. Sruthisagar Yamunan, 'Following the Flood,' *The Hindu*, 12 December 2015.
39. A. Ranganathan, 'Viable Project or White Elephant,' *Business Line*, 13 August 2008.
40. 'Kids Sat Waiting, Parents Found Dead in Pile of Bodies After 5 Days,' *The Times of India*, 10 December 2015.
41. Edwin Arnold, *India Revisited*, Trubner, 1886, p. 258.
42. Raveena Joseph, 'The Storm Chaser,' *The Hindu*, 11 December 2015.
43. B. Aravind Kumar and S. Rukmini, 'Freak Weather Whipped Up a Perfect Storm,' *The Hindu*, 7 December 2015.
44. 'Yunus Rescued Them from Chennai Floods, They Named Their Baby After Him,' *India Today*, 9 December 2015.
45. Arun Janardhanan, 'Chennai Floods: The Day City Went Under, Who Did What—and Who Did Not,' *The Indian Express*, 25 April 2019.
46. 'Sterlite Protesters Shot In Head, Chest—Many From Back, Says Report,' *NDTV*, 22 December 2018.
47. Tarique Anwar, 'Were the Chennai Floods a Government-made Disaster?,' *Firstpost*, 14 December, 2015
48. Dhanya Rajendran and S. Ramanathan, 'Chennai Floods: What Happened at Chembarambakkam, Negligence or Nature's Fury?,' *The News Minute*, 9 December 2015.
49. 'The Hindu Not Published for First Time Since 1878,' *BBC News*, 2 December 2015.
50. S. Mohamed Imranullah, 'Till 2011, Sasikala Had a Big Role in Government and AIADMK, Says Her Niece Krishnapriya,' *The Hindu*, 24 March 2018.
51. 'Tax Officials Find Secret Letter On The Gutka Scam In Sasikala's Room,' Press Trust of India, 13 January 2018.

52. K.V. Lakshmana, 'Jayalalitha No-show at Kalam's Funeral Triggers Health Concern,' *Hindustan Times*, 30 July 2015.
53. 'Disaster in Chennai Caused by the Torrential Rains and Consequent Flooding,' Department-related Parliamentary Committee on Home Affairs, tabled in the parliament on 12 August 2016.
54. 'Skeleton Found in Chennai May Be of December 2015 Flood Victim,' *The Times of India*, 26 April 2018.
55. Now Chennai struggles to lay its dead to rest, Arun Janardhanan, December 10, 2015
56. Shalini Nair, 'Unprecedented Calamity, Chennai Toll 269, Says Rajnath Singh,' *The Indian Express*, 4 December 2015.
57. Pheba Mathew, 'Shunted Out and Neglected By Govt, Poor Continue to Suffer in Semmenchery,' *The News Minute*, 9 December 2015; Sibi Arasu, 'We Had to Pay a Bribe to Cremate Our Mother,' *BBC News*, 16 December 2015.
58. 'Chennai–Mangalore Express Train Derails in Tamil Nadu, At Least 39 Injured,' *News18*, 4 September 2015.
59. '35 Dead Bodies Bought To Royapettah Govt Hospital, 15 Dead in Private Hospital,' *Thanthi TV*, 4 December 2015.
60. T.A. Johnson, '48 Hours at the MIOT Hospital Where 18 Died,' *The Indian Express*, 5 December 2015.
61. 'Hospital, Govt Authorities Play Blame Game As 14 Patients Lose Their Lives,' *Firstpost*, 4 December 2015.
62. Anil Srinivasan, 'Ragas in the Rain: Playing the Blues in Flood-wrecked Chennai,' *Scroll.in*, 18 December 2015.
63. 'In Flooded Chennai, a Woman Sits With Mother's Body for Nearly 20 Hours,' *NDTV*, 3 December 2015.
64. Arun Janardhanan, 'Now Chennai Struggles to Lay its Dead to Rest,' *The Indian Express*, 10 December 2015.
65. G.C. Shekhar, 'Long Wait for the Dead,' *The Telegraph*, 6 December 2015.
66. 'Excavations and Research at the Palaeolithic Site of Attirampakkam,' Sharma Centre For Heritage Education, sharmaheritage.com/projects/attirampakkam.

67. Sarah Iqbal, 'Ancient Stone Tools Found in Tamil Nadu Push Back "Out of Africa" Exodus Date,' *The Wire*, 2 February 2018.
68. R. Sivakumar, 'After Keezhadi, Tiruvallur Site in Line for Excavation,' *The New Indian Express*, 19 February 2019.
69. Charles Stewart Crole, *The Chingleput, Late Madras, District*, Lawrence Asylum Press, 1879, p. 196.
70. Ibid., p. 194.
71. *Macmillan's Magazine*, vol. 37 (November 1877–April 1878), pp. 249–250.
72. 'Ennore Creek,' The Story of Ennore. storyofennore.wordpress.com/about/ennore-creek/.
73. 'An Open Letter to Declare Ennore Creek as a Climate Sanctuary Save Chennai; Save Ennore Creek,' The Coastal Resource Centre, 16 June 2017.
74. *Manual of the Administration of the Madras Presidency*, vol. 2 (1885), p. 94.
75. Nityanand Jayaraman, 'Chennai's Fishermen's Call to Residents: Join Our Campaign to Save Ennore Creek, Save Our City,' 2 September 2016.
76. Nityanand Jayaraman and Pooja Kumar, 'A Venice that No Longer Is: Remembering the Canals of North Madras,' *The Hindu*, 29 August 2017.
77. 'Death by a Thousand Cuts: Report of Public Hearing Held On Loss of Ecology and Fisher Livelihood in Ennore Creek,' April 2016.
78. Karthikeyan Hemalatha, 'Panel Recommends Moratorium on Industrial Expansion in Ennore to Save Polluted Water Bodies,' *The Times of India*, 18 April 2016.
79. Akhila Kannadasan, 'Flood of Kindness as the Skies Open Up,' *The Hindu*, 2 December 2015.
80. To recreate the Buckingham Canal story I relied on the following sources: Florence Nightingale, 'Irrigation and Water Transit in India,' *Illustrated London News*, 1879; John Allen Moore, *Baptist Mission Portraits*, Smyth & Helwys Publishing, 1994; Emma

Rauschenbusch Clough, *John E. Clough: Missionary to the Telugus of South India,* American Bapt. Missionary Union, 1902.

81. Prasannan Parthasarathi, 'Forest and a New Energy Economy in Nineteenth-Century South India,' in (ed.) Gareth Austin, *Economic Development and Environmental History in the Anthropocene*, Bloomsbury, 2017.
82. Moore, *Baptist Mission Portraits.*
83. Siddharth Prabhakar, 'Locked At Home, Armyman, Wife Died Sending SOS,' *The Times of India,* 9 December 2015.
84. The narikurava or kuruvikaran community is involved in making rosaries and beaded jewellery traditionally. After a long struggle, the community received the Scheduled Tribe status in 2016.
85. S. Muthiah, *Tales of Old and New Madras: The Dalliance of Miss Mansell and 34 Other Stories of 350 Years,* Affiliated East-West Press, Chennai, 1989.
86. Frank Penny, *Fort St George, Madras: A Short History of Our First Possession in India,* Swan Sonnenschein, London, 1900, p. 7.
87. Henry Davison Love, *Vestiges of Old Madras 1640–1800: Vol 1,* Government of India, 1913, p. 86.
88. *The Madras Tercentenary Commemoration Volume,* Oxford University Press, 4 August 1939, p. 35.
89. Priya Baskaran, 'Preface' in *The Gods of the Holy Koovam,* Aalayam Kanden Trust, Chennai.
90. N.S. Ramaswami, *Political History of Carnatic under the Nawabs,* Abhinav Publications, p. 320.
91. Penny, *Fort St George, Madras.*
92. Florence Nightingale, *Sanitary State of the Army in India,* London E Stanford, 1863, p. 55
93. V. Sriram, 'How Florence Nightingale Got Madras its Drains,' *The Hindu,* 8 January 2013.
94. Florence Nightingale, 'Letters to the Editor,' *The Illustrated London News,* 28 April 1879.
95. Nightingale, *Sanitary State of the Army in India,* p. 92.

96. V. Lakshmana, 'Chennai's Municipal Workers Mobilise to Begin Mammoth Clean-up,' *Hindustan Times*, 9 December 2015.
97. 'Tsunami to 2015 Floods: No Respite for Dalits in Disaster Response, Tamil Nadu,' National Dalit Watch–National Campaign on Dalit Human Rights, New Delhi, with Social Awareness Society for Youth, Tamil Nadu, dalits.nl/pdf/NoRespiteForDalitsInDisasterResponse.pdf.
98. 'Inadequate Civic Amenities for Sanitation Workers in Chennai Flood Cleanup,' Thozhilalar Koodam, 15 December 2015, tnlabour.in/news/2947.
99. Sruthisagar Yamunan, 'Thousands of Residents Flee North Chennai,' *The Hindu*, 3 December 2015.
100. Janani Sampath, 'Transgenders Say They Have Been Shunned by Relief Groups,' DTNext, 13 December 2015.
101. 'Caste Discrimination in Relief, Tamil Nadu Floods 2015,' *Economic & Political Weekly*, vol. 51, no. 2 (9 Jan 2016).
102. 'Equality in Aid, Addressing Caste Discrimination in Humanitarian Response,' IDSN, September 2013.
103. 'Sustainable and Resilient Communities: A Profile of Dalits in Disaster Risk Reduction in South Asia,' Asia Dalit Rights Forum, pp. 3–4.
104. Sujata Mody, 'While Chennai's Sanitation Workers Help the Deluged City, Who's Looking After Them?' *Scroll.in*, 3 Dec 2015, scroll.in/article/773230/while-chennais-sanitation-workers-help-the-deluged-city-whos-looking-after-them.
105. Madras Legislative Assembly Debates, 1937.
106. Madras Legislative Assembly Debates, 1946.
107. Madras Legislative Council Debates, 1967.
108. V. Sriram, 'Why is it 'Sink'ara Chennai?,' Madras Heritage and Carnatic Music, 9 November 2012, sriramv.wordpress.com/2012/11/09/why-is-it-sinkara-chennai/.
109. C.S. Srinivasachari, *The History of the City of Madras*, P. Varadachary and Co., 1939.
110. S. Muthiah, *Madras Rediscovered, East West*, p. 156.

111. 'M. K. Stalin Digs Out Special CAG Report on 2015 Floods, Puts Govt in Hot Water,' *The Times of India*, 23 March, 2018.
112. William Digby, *The Famine Campaign in Southern India*, Longman Green and Co., 1878, pp. 148–149.
113. 'Report of the Comptroller and Auditor General of India: Flood Management and Response in Chennai and Its Suburban Areas,' p. x.
114. The PWD issued Casa Grande developers an NOC subject to condition that the site should be filled with a height varying from 3.40 m to 3.95 m to avoid inundation; a setback of 9 m should be left on the northern side and eastern side and a pucca compound wall should be constructed all along the inner site boundary to avoid erosion in the site in future.
115. Order in WP (MD) No 7855 of 2019 dated 3 April 2019.

Acknowledgements

Thank you to:

Swaroop, my companion, for picking up after me, every single day, while I worked on this book. For reading every draft, for researching the floods just as much as I did, and for being my own personal cheerleader. For the unwavering support from the time of the floods to all the nights and days of tears and anger during the making of this book. And the love.

Roshan Balasubramanian for the generosity, for sharing an incredible amount of information and fighting the good fight where it matters the most.

Interviewees featured in this book for sharing their experiences and pain.

H.S. Hredai, Prashanth Kiran and G. Jothi for helping with the filing of crucial RTIs and following up diligently until answers emerged from various departments.

Coastal Resource Centre and Pooja Kumar for making a difference to our city and for all the resources that went into making this book.

Poongkhulali Balasubramanian for helping me understand the legal issues plaguing Ennore, for accompanying me on the toxic tour early one morning and for all the bondas, coffee and her company.

Journalists who covered the floods in TN upon whose work I have relied a great deal.

Jayapriya Vasudevan for being an amazing agent–friend. For believing in me. For bringing my dreams to fruition.

Toto Funds the Arts and Sangam House for giving me the most beautiful setting to write this book in, as part of the Toto Sangam House Residency Fellowship 2016.

Nrityagram's earthy serene grounds, fantastic company and moka pot coffee.

The Jayanti Residency for the lovely cottage in Ranikhet overlooking the Trishul, where I wrote some parts of this book.

Everyone at Westland who made this book possible, especially G.S. Ajitha for her vision and Janani Ganesan for her patience and rigour. Also, proofreader Vidhi Bhargava for bringing the best version of this book out and art director Vishwajyoti Ghosh for making it look great.

Anita Nair for the great support, honest feedback and the honour of her mentor-ship.

Arvind Subramanian, a besotted Chennaiite, for showing keen interest in this book on his hometown.

T.M. Krishna for reading an early draft of this book.

Raj Prambi for the daily reminders that I am supposed to thank him in this book.

Balajee for telling me over coffee one day at Apoorva's Sangeetha that life can be measured in ways other than my to-do list.

Subadra for the kindest email that came to me in the April of 2017, while working on some of the most depressing parts of this book.

My parents for showing me what courage means, by recovering from the floods and moving on most admirably.

Sharan for his timely support for this book and in life.

Aarthi for being there through everything. The only constant I have known apart from family is our love and friendship.

Sriya for the coffee sessions and introducing me to OfERR's work.

Manju and Krishnaveni for the nurture through these years.

All those who volunteered in 2015 and helped bring my city and its people back to life from the brink of despair.

Saroja and Golden Chariot, for serving us before being lost to the floods.